CUSTOM CURRICULUM

The Drug Free Challenge

Jim Marian

teacher training by
**Stephen Arterburn and
Marv Penner**

options by
**Rick Bundschuh,
Rev. Nelson E. Copeland, Jr.,
Kara Eckmann Powell,
Christian Hill,
Joel Lusz,
Jim Marian,
Ginny Olson,
Marv Penner,
Glenn Procopio, and
Joel Walker**

Cook Ministry Resources
a division of Cook Communications Ministries
Colorado Springs, Colorado/Paris, Ontario

**Custom Curriculum
The Drug Free Challenge**

©1998 David C. Cook
Church Ministries

All rights reserved. Except for the student sheets and parent pages, which may be copied for ministry use, no part of this book may be reproduced in any form without the written permission of the publisher, unless otherwise noted in the text.

Unless otherwise noted, Scripture quotations are from the Holy Bible, New International Version (NIV), ©1973, 1978, 1984 by International Bible Society. Used by permission of Zondervan Bible Publishers.

Series Creator: John Duckworth

Editor: Rick Wesselhoff

Series Designer: Bill Paetzold

Additional design:
Sonya Duckworth, Erica Whitcombe

Cover and Inside Illustrator:
Jim Starr

Special thanks to Joel Lusz, Matt Winzenreid, and Christian Hill for their Resource page contributions.

Published by
Cook Ministry Resources,
a division of
Cook Communications Ministries
4050 Lee Vance View,
Colorado Springs, CO
80918-7100

www.cookministries.com

Colorado Springs, Colorado/
Paris, Ontario

Printed in U.S.A
ISBN: 0-7814-5459-X

The CUSTOM CURRICULUM Challenge
We Challenge You to ...

▶ *Refuse "canned" curriculum.*

> Don't be boxed into one way of doing things.

▶ *Think about your group.*

> How do your students learn best? What kinds of goals do you have for your group? You know what will work with your students.

▶ *Reach your teens.*

> Don't just fill up an hour of programming.

It takes a few minutes each week to customize your curriculum. But if you're willing to take the challenge, the payoff is lessons that work—not just on paper, but with real, live teens. With *your* teens.

CONTENTS

ABOUT THE AUTHORS 4
HOW TO CUSTOMIZE YOUR CURRICULUM 5
PUBLICITY CLIP ART 8
TALKING TO TEENS ABOUT DRUGS AND ALCOHOL 11
DRUGS AND ALCOHOL, A PARENTAL EYE-OPENER 13

1. BUT I DON'T WANT TO MISS OUT ON THE FUN! — 14
What Jesus has to offer and why it's better than the "fun" of drugs and alcohol.

2. COPING WITH LIFE IN A COP-OUT CULTURE — 30
Life's tough, but God wants us to do more than give in to drugs and alcohol.

3. BUT IT'S NOT THAT EASY TO "JUST SAY NO" — 46
Four Bible-based strategies that work.

4. GLAZED EYES, HANGOVERS, AND, UH . . . REALLY GREAT PRAYER TIMES — 62
The effects of drugs and alcohol on the "temple of the Holy Spirit."

5. THROWING THE LIFE PRESERVER — 78
Using Jesus' model for confronting a friend if he or she has a problem.

About the Authors

Jim Marian
5 sessions, Fellowship and Worship, and Large Group options

Jim's 15 years of youth ministry experience include 10 as the high school pastor at Lake Avenue Congregational Church in Pasadena. In addition, he has led many retreats, conferences, and training seminars. Jim is an expert on teaching teens how to worship. His books include *Worship Services for Youth Groups* and *Leading Your Students in Worship*.

Marv Penner
Heard It All Before options

Marv is the chairman of the youth ministry and counseling departments at Briercrest Schools Seminary in Caronport, Saskatchewan. He also runs the Canadian Center for Adolescent Research and is a popular speaker, seminar leader, and author. He has also written *Parent Pains* in the Custom Curriculum series.

Joel Walker
Extra Action, Mostly Guys options

Joel runs Peak 3, a high adventure ropes course and initiative games ministry center in Colorado Springs that draws visitors from around the U.S. Joel is a 15-year veteran of youth ministry and an expert in using initiative games for Christian ministry.

Kara Eckmann Powell
Combined options

In her spare time after writing, speaking, and studying for her doctorate in Practical Theology, Kara is the part-time college pastor at Lake Avenue Congregational Church in Pasadena. Her books include *The Word on the Old Testament* (with Jim Burns). Her strengths include the ability to make abstract truths concrete and practical for teens.

Rev. Nelson E. Copeland, Jr.
Urban options

Nelson is the President of the Christian Education Coalition for African-American Leadership, an organization dedicated to reinforcing educational and cultural excellence for urban teenagers. His books include *Great Games for City Kids* and *A New Agenda for Urban Youth*. He has 13 years of youth ministry experience and currently leads a youth ministry in Baltimore.

Rick Bundschuh
Extra Fun, Little Bible Background options

Rick is one of the true innovators in youth ministry today. What else would you call a guy who's invented youth ministry classics like "Noodle Jousting" and "The Chocolate Vacuum"? In his spare time after surfing, kayaking, and climbing volcanoes—as well as speaking and writing many books for youth ministry—Rick enjoys pastoring a church in Kauai, Hawaii (somebody's got to do it!).

Ginny Olson
Mostly Girls options

Ginny is the director of youth ministry at North Park Seminary in suburban Chicago. Her 15 years of youth ministry experience included 10 years at Willow Creek Community Church, where she oversaw ministry to junior high girls. Ginny was a contributing author to the book *Breaking the Gender Barrier in Youth Ministry* and is the executive director of the Organization of Women in Youth Ministry.

Joel Lusz
Media options

Joel is a 15-year veteran of youth ministry whose strengths include creativity with home video. In addition to serving as a minister to youth and their families in south Florida, Joel runs Video Nonsense Ministries, a vehicle for his creative and hilarious home videos for use in youth ministry.

Glenn Procopio
Extra Challenge options

Glenn is the director of discipleship for his denomination, North Cleveland Church of God, and the youth pastor at his church in Tennessee. Glenn has also written a book of devotionals for youth workers and *Ministry in a Box*.

Christian Hill
Small Group options

Christian formerly served on staff at Saddleback Community Church, where his responsibilities included student small groups and worship. Christian recently built a youth ministry from the ground up in Colorado Springs and he consults with other youth workers about how to build ministries from scratch.

How to Customize your Curriculum

All right, you may be thinking. With all of these options flying around, how do I put a session together? I don't have a lot of time, you know. We know! That's why we've made Custom Curriculum as easy as possible.

1. Read the basic lesson plan.

Every Custom Curriculum session in this book has four or five steps designed to meet five goals. It's important to understand these five goals as you choose the options for your group.

GETTING TOGETHER
The goal for Getting Together is to break the ice. It may involve a fun way to introduce the lesson.

GETTING THIRSTY
The goal for Getting Thirsty is to earn students' interest before you dive into the Bible. Why should students care about your topic? Why should they care what the Bible has to say about it? This will motivate your students to dig deeper.

GETTING THE WORD
The goal for Getting the Word is to find out what God has to say about the topic they care about. By exploring and discussing carefully-selected passages, you'll help students find out how God's Word applies to their lives.

GETTING THE POINT
The goal for Getting the Point is to make the leap from ideals and principles to real-world situations students are likely to face. It may involve practicing biblical principles with case studies or roleplays.

GETTING PERSONAL
The goal for Getting Personal is to help each group member respond to the lesson with a specific action. What should group members do as a result of this session? This step will help each person find a specific "next step" response that works for him or her.

2. Consider your options.

Every Custom Curriculum session gives you 14 different types of options. How do you choose? First, take a look at the list of option categories below. Then spend some time thinking and praying about your group. How do your students learn best? What kind of goals have you set for your group? Put a check mark by the options that you're most interested in.

Extra Action—for groups that like physical challenges and learn better when they're moving, interacting, and experiencing the lesson.

Media—to spice up your meeting with video, music, or other popular media.

Heard It All Before—for fresh approaches that get past the defenses of students who are jaded by years in church.

Little Bible Background—to use when most of your students are strangers to the Bible or haven't yet made a Christian commitment.

Extra Fun—for longer, more "festive" youth meetings where additional emphasis is put on having fun.

Fellowship and Worship—for building deeper relationships or enabling students to praise God together.

Mostly Girls—to address girls' concerns and to substitute activities girls might prefer.

Mostly Guys—to address guys' concerns and to substitute activities guys might prefer.

Small Group—for adapting activities that might be tough with groups of fewer than eight students.

Large Group—to alter steps for groups of more than 20 students.

Urban—for fitting sessions to urban facilities and multiethnic (especially African-American) concerns.

Short Meeting Time—Tips for condensing the meeting. The standard meeting is designed to last 45 to 60 minutes. These include options to cut, replace, or trim time off the standard steps.

Combined Junior High/High School—to use when you're mixing age levels but an activity or case study would be too "young" or "old" for part of the group.

Sixth Grade—appearing only in junior high/middle school volumes, this option helps you change steps that sixth graders might find hard to understand or related to.

Extra Challenge—appearing only in high school volumes, this option lets you crank up the voltage for students who are ready for more Scripture or more demanding personal application.

3 Find your options.

We've included a sample lesson page here. The side notes will show you just how easy it is to find the options you're looking for. Watch for the options you're interested in to show up in the sidebars, like the one below.

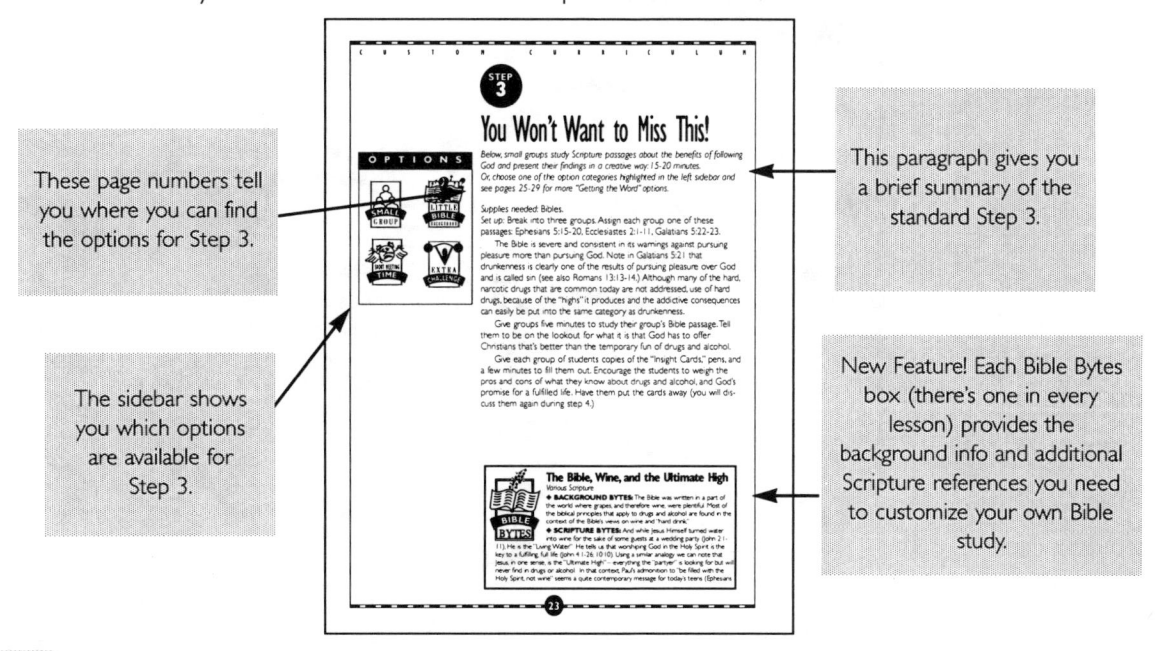

These page numbers tell you where you can find the options for Step 3.

This paragraph gives you a brief summary of the standard Step 3.

The sidebar shows you which options are available for Step 3.

New Feature! Each Bible Bytes box (there's one in every lesson) provides the background info and additional Scripture references you need to customize your own Bible study.

4 Customize your curriculum!

When you turn to the back of each session, you'll see five options pages that look something like this.

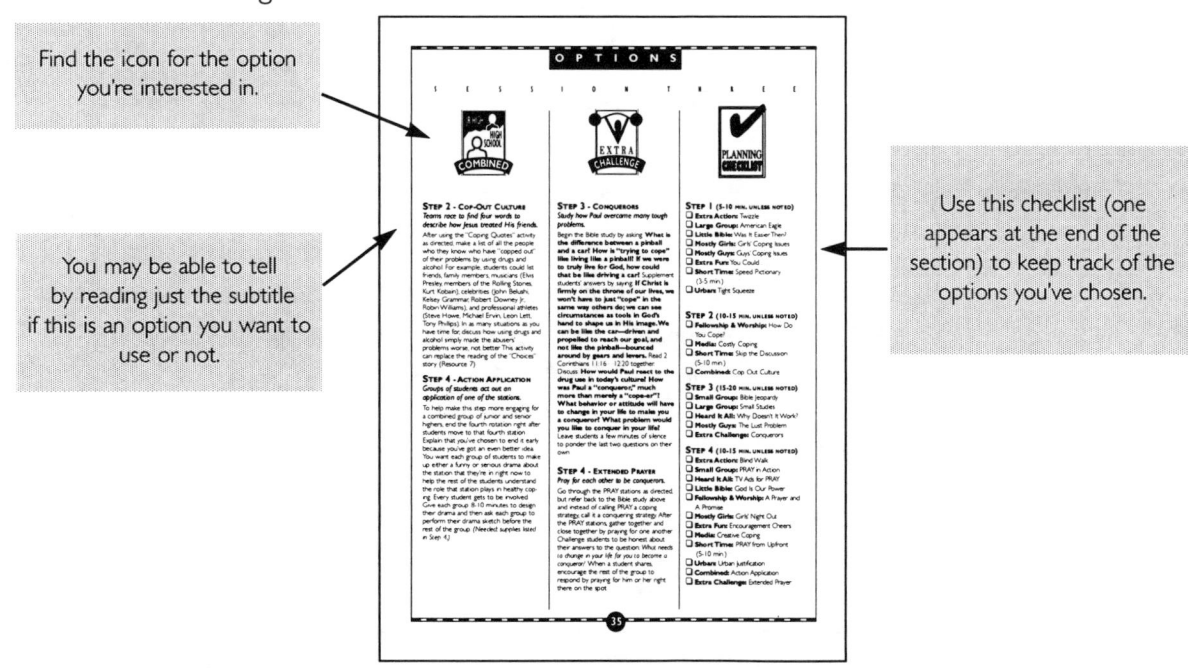

Find the icon for the option you're interested in.

You may be able to tell by reading just the subtitle if this is an option you want to use or not.

Use this checklist (one appears at the end of the section) to keep track of the options you've chosen.

Publicity Clip Art

The images on these two pages are designed to help you promote this course within your church and community. Feel free to photocopy anything here and adapt it to fit your publicity needs. This page could be used as a flier that you send or hand out to kids—or as a bulletin insert. The art on the next page could be used to add visual interest to newsletters, calendars, bulletin boards, or other promotions. Be creative and have fun!

"It's JUST a beer. What's the big deal?"

"It'll help you relax..."

"WOW! What a buzz!"

You've seen the stats. You've heard the stories. You know what drugs and alcohol can do to your body—you know what they can do to your life. But you also have questions. Real questions. Like: **What's wrong with experimenting a little?** and **Why should I miss out on the fun?** Get some real answers to your real questions. Find out what The Drug Free Challenge is all about.

WHERE:

WHEN:

QUESTIONS? CALL:

LIFE is tough.
HOW DO YOU COPE?

You've heard the slogan "JUST SAY NO!" but HOW do you say no in the real world?

The Drug Free CHALLENGE

why be DRUG FREE?

Ever feel like you're MISSING THE PARTY?

Teacher Training/Parent Pieces

"Why Not?"
by Stephen Arterburn

There are two important questions today's Christian teens must answer every single day. "Why wait?" and "Why not?" Why Wait? deals with waiting for sex until marriage. The Why not? question goes something like this: If drugs and alcohol make me feel good and if everybody else is doing it, why not? Both questions are very enticing to a young person looking for a rite of passage and a sense of belonging. Any youth worker or parent not prepared to address these questions is missing an opportunity to connect with a teen and perhaps help him or her avoid years of heartache.

Through campaigns like *True Love Waits*, *Thru the Roof*, and *Why Wait?*, youth workers have focused large amounts of time and energy with great success to equip and motivate their students to wait until marriage for sex. The same cannot be said about the second question. It is probably more of a stigma on today's high school campus to have never tasted alcohol than it is to be a virgin. The average high school student may have three times as many opportunities to try drugs or alcohol as they do opportunities to have sex. Yet, many youth workers often give their students a quick "Just Say No" pep talk and think they've prepared them to face the real world. It's time that youth workers begin to pour large amounts of time and energy to equip and motivate today's teens to be drug free.

You know that students' needs are complex. They won't be helped by quick fixes. They are hungry for real answers to real questions. As you strive to provide them, you can keep two things in mind. First, rely on the insights and ideas in this book. This is not just another "Just Say No" pep talk. It's an important work that features a team effort from a number of seasoned youth ministry veterans. But second, remember that the most important thing you can give your students is something you can't find in any book—your own story. Use the following two pages to help you prepare to talk to your teens about your own experience.

We encourage your work on the "front lines" with students. You will never know the full impact of your work. You may be the only person to discuss this important subject with a teenager. You may be the only person to show love for hurting teens—and that may be the very thing that leads some of your students to say no to drugs and alcohol and yes to Jesus Christ. You will never know the tally of your work. Do not give up on a frustrating and sometimes difficult problem. You can and will make a difference.

An Important Note: Working with Parents

There is only so much you can do for your students. The most important job is for the parents. Many studies show that the key factor in whether a teen says no to drugs and alcohol is whether they have a close, emotional bond with a parent. It is the parent, not the church, or school that must play the key role in kids making wise decisions. The greatest thing you can do to combat drugs and alcohol is to encourage parents to love their kids. FEEL FREE TO PHOTOCOPY THE FOLLOWING THREE PAGES AND SEND THEM OUT TO YOUR STUDENTS' PARENTS. This important information will help you partner with and encourage parents.

Talking to Teens about Drugs and Alcohol

The best way to gain credibility in the area of drugs and alcohol is to tell teens that you know how tempting it is to want to experiment. Curiosity and a strong desire to experience the unknown lead many teens to try alcohol and drugs. Do not downplay that urge. Rather, relate to it and acknowledge that it would be easy for anyone to give in.

Your Story

There are really only two options you can take in a discussion on this temptation. You either have to explain why you succumbed to the temptation yourself and the effect of it, or you can talk of how you refused to succumb and the way that made you feel. There is a third option and many take it, but lying about your past is never recommended.

Let's look at how you would approach alcohol and drugs if your only option was to tell how you gave in to peer pressure. The following are some concepts to stress when relating your story:
1. It was not all it was cracked up to be.
2. It was not worth breaking the law just to be able to feel part of a group.
3. The act was done out of weakness, not strength.
4. The decision to drink and/or try drugs was a symptom of a character weakness that manifested itself in other areas.
5. You admire others who do not need a substance to feel better about themselves.

If you are able to tell how you resisted peer pressure, talk about:
1. How you felt about yourself.
2. The admiration others had (and have) for you.
3. How the strength to say no carried over and helped you in other areas of your life.
4. Other things that were more tempting or just as tempting and how you handled them.
5. How the students can follow your example.

Risks and Rewards

Once you have entered the discussion, there are two concepts that need to be addressed: risk and reward. Talk with teens about the rewards (or benefits) that they believe they might obtain if they tried alcohol or drugs. The list may include such things as:
1. Feeling part of the group.
2. Feeling grown up or mature.
3. Experiencing something new.
4. The accomplishment of getting away with something.
5. Feeling intoxicated.
6. Relief from emotional pain.
7. Feeling more comfortable with friends.

These are some of the reasons teens try alcohol and drugs. Talking about these reasons won't make them seem any more appealing. In fact, discussing them takes some of the power away from them. It's especially helpful if teens realize that they are not the only ones who feel that way. Tempting desires are less alluring when we know that others have felt the same way or desired the same things.

After discussing the appeal or reward, risk needs to be addressed. It is in this area that you can provide insight that many teens often overlook. Clarifying the risks for teens can be a powerful deterrent. When discussing risk, be sure to include the following:
1. Risk of being caught.
2. Risk of being punished.
3. Risk of getting hooked or addicted.
4. Risk of feeling worse about yourself.
5. Risk of losing control and getting hurt.
6. Risk of stepping outside of God's will.
7. Risk of hurting someone else.
8. Risk of leading someone else down the wrong path.
9. Risk of becoming "numb" and unable to handle pain or tough problems.

Help teens name the risks and explore all the dimensions of each one. Ask teens to share the consequences they have seen in the lives of those who chose to drink or use drugs.

The Rewards of Saying No

You can discuss the many rewards of not using drugs or alcohol. These include:
1. Self-discipline
2. Self-respect
3. Self-control
4. Following God; seeking His will
5. Character development
6. Being seen as a leader
7. Respect from other others

You can essentially sum up all the rewards of abstaining by discussing the following: Whenever anyone drinks or takes drugs, he or she does it to feel good. It might make him or her feel more comfortable with a certain group of peers, or it may be simply because the chemical causes one to feel good physically. But making decisions as a mature person requires that you go beyond what makes you feel good *now* and choose what will make you feel good about yourself *later*. Beyond this, mature Christians consider what is right and wrong. Not only do they want to feel good about themselves, they want to feel right about themselves. Only in doing the right thing can we feel right about ourselves . . . and what a feeling that is!

Stephen Arterburn

Cofounder,

Minirth Meier New Life Clinics

Drugs and Alcohol, A Parental Eye-opener

As parents we have a responsibility to care for the health and well-being of our children. Sometimes it feels like there's a fine line between being an observant, responsive parent and just being paranoid. Here are some signals to watch for to help you determine whether your son or daughter may have a drug or alcohol problem. Please note that some of the patterns described below could point to other struggles your teenager might be experiencing. Either way the symptoms described below should not be ignored. They're all unhealthy and a wise parent will pay close attention.

1. **Mood swings that go beyond the normal ups and downs of adolescent transitions.** Look for extremes, both high and low, that appear to unconnected to visible circumstances or events in your teen's life.

2. **Problems at school.** Dropping grades, disinterest in sports or other activities, and, of course, skipping school or missing classes are all signals that should be taken seriously.

3. **Choosing unhealthy friendships.** Be careful not to judge teenagers who look or dress differently too quickly, but realize that friendships with kids who abuse drugs and alcohol can make it very tough for your son or daughter to stay committed to their standards.

4. **Habitual dishonesty.** Adolescents who abuse drugs and alcohol have no choice but to "live a lie." Often the lying habit becomes so familiar that they lie or distort the truth even when it's not necessary.

5. **Isolation and secrecy.** Teens who disengage from their families to spend most of their time alone in their room and those who become inappropriately defensive when asked about their plans or activities may very well have something significant to hide. Beware when kids go straight to their rooms when they arrive home.

6. **Violence, vandalism, and delinquency.** A tendency to be destructive, angry, and violent is often connected with drug and alcohol abuse. Note signs of cuts and bruises that may indicate having been in a fight and take very seriously any brushes your son or daughter may have with the law.

7. **Stealing.** Illegal substances are expensive and most students don't have the kind of cash it takes to support a drug or alcohol habit. Watch for things missing around the house or for items in your adolescent's possession that may not belong to them.

8. **Drugs or alcohol missing.** Keep a close watch on your medicine cabinet if it contains prescription drugs that could be abused. The same principle is true for your refrigerator, liquor cabinet, or wine cellar. Too many teens have learned to drink or abuse drugs in the lonely convenience of their own homes when no one was paying attention.

9. **Physical symptoms.** These may be very obvious but for some reason parents often choose to deny or ignore physical symptoms. Glazed eyes, insomnia, hallucinations, slurred speech, alcohol breath, needle marks, and the smell of marijuana smoke on clothing cannot be rationalized away.

10. **Stashed drugs and alcohol.** Finding bottles, baggies, drug paraphernalia or unusual powders and substances in drawers, pockets, backpacks, or hiding places must be addressed directly. Be prepared for excuses and explanations (see #4) but recognize that these sins are serious and must be confronted.

Facing the awful reality that our kids may have a serious problem is not easy for most parents. You may want to enlist the help of a counselor, pastor, or youth worker if you feel that you need to confront this issue in your family. Whatever you do, don't belittle the problem by assuming that it's just an adolescent phase or rite of passage. It IS a big deal and must be treated as such.

Marv Penner
Chairman, Department of Counseling
Briercrest Schools Seminary, Saskatchewan

SESSION 1
But I Don't Want to Miss Out On the Fun!

YOUR GOALS FOR THIS SESSION:
Choose one or more

☐ To help students realize that experimenting with drugs and alcohol has both physical and spiritual consequences.

☐ To help students understand that there are several ways to view the "fun" of drug and alcohol use.

☐ To help students understand that being filled with God's Spirit is ultimately more satisfying than being temporarily filled with drugs and alcohol.

☐ Other: _____

Your Bible Base:

Ephesians 5:15-20
Ecclesiastes 2:1-11
Galatians 5:22-25

STEP 1

Drug and Alcohol Effects

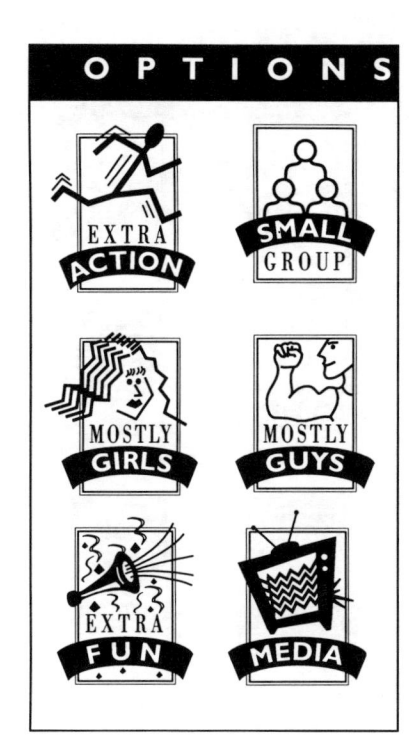

"Drug Effects" is a game where teams race to list the many kinds of effects drugs and alcohol can have on humans: 10 minutes.
Or, choose one of the option categories highlighted in the left sidebar and see pages 25-29 for more "Getting Together" options.

OPTIONS
- EXTRA ACTION
- SMALL GROUP
- MOSTLY GIRLS
- MOSTLY GUYS
- EXTRA FUN
- MEDIA

Supplies needed: pens and paper.
Set up: Break into teams of two or three and hand out paper and pens.

Before you dive into a series on drugs and alcohol, one of the first things you'll need to do is see what your students know about these drugs' effects. Give teams the category "drug effects" and two minutes to list as many kinds of effects drugs, both legal and illegal, have on humans. After the two minutes are up, have teams read their lists to the group one answer at a time. Cross off any answers that any other team also listed. Award teams one point for each answer that no other team came up with.

What are some positive effects drugs have on us?
(Prescription drugs heal us, control pain, etc.)

What are some negative effects drugs have on us?
(Impaired judgement, addiction, put us and others at risk.)

A drug is a substance that effects your body, either positively or negatively. But keep in mind that drugs are not always pills. Alcohol, tobacco and nicotine are also classified as drugs.

Why are some people drawn to drugs and alcohol? Does it make their life better or worse?

Be sure to differentiate between legal and illegal drugs for your students. Also remind them that although alcohol is legal, it cannot be legally consumed until they turn 21!

SESSION ONE

STEP 2

Drugs and Alcohol Talkstarter

Below, students use a talkstarter resource to discuss drug use: 10-15 minutes. Or, choose one of the option categories highlighted in the right sidebar and see pages 25-29 for more "Getting Thirsty" options.

Supplies needed: copies of Resource 1, pencils.
Set up: Hand out copies of "Drugs and Alcohol Talkstarter" (Resource 1, page 20) and pencils.

Discuss the talkstarter questions one at a time. Every student can follow along by filling out his or her own sheet. No student should feel *obligated* to answer out loud, but the talkstarter is designed with provoking questions to engage your students in lively discussion. Listen to all of your students' points of view, even if they differ from your own or from the Bible. *There will be time to discuss these issues in light of the Bible's ultimate authority. But first it's important to communicate that everyone's opinion matters.*

To conclude, say: **We live in a world that says, "If it feels good, do it!" As a result, many people see nothing wrong with drugs or alcohol. They think, "What's wrong with experimenting a little bit if it makes me feel better?" But what should our response as Christians be? If we really do know Jesus personally, should we expect drugs and alcohol to meet our needs? How much fun do they offer? Is what God offers better?**

OPTIONS

- LARGE GROUP
- HEARD IT ALL BEFORE
- FELLOWSHIP & WORSHIP
- MEDIA
- SHORT MEETING TIME
- JR. HIGH / HIGH SCHOOL COMBINED

STEP 3

You Won't Want to Miss This!

Below, small groups study Scripture passages about the benefits of following God and present their findings in a creative way: 15-20 minutes.
Or, choose one of the option categories highlighted in the left sidebar and see pages 25-29 for more "Getting the Word" options.

OPTIONS: Small Group, Little Bible Background, Short Meeting Time, Extra Challenge

Supplies needed: Bibles.
Set up: Break into three groups. Assign each group one of these passages: Ephesians 5:15-20, Ecclesiastes 2:1-11, Galatians 5:22-23.

The Bible is severe and consistent in its warnings against pursuing pleasure more than pursuing God. Note in Galatians 5:21 that drunkenness is clearly one of the results of pursuing pleasure over God and is called sin (see also Romans 13:13-14.) Although many of the hard, narcotic drugs that are common today are not addressed, use of hard drugs, because of the "highs" it produces and the addictive consequences can easily be put into the same category as drunkenness.

Give groups five minutes to study their group's Bible passage. Tell them to be on the lookout for what it is that God has to offer Christians that's better than the temporary fun of drugs and alcohol.

Give each group of students copies of the "Insight Cards," pens, and a few minutes to fill them out. Encourage the students to weigh the pros and cons of what they know about drugs and alcohol, and God's promise for a fulfilled life. Have them put the cards away (you will discuss them again during step 4.)

Then, give the groups a few more minutes to prepare a presentation or roleplay that advertises the benefits of their Scripture passage.

The Bible, Wine, and the Ultimate High
Various Scripture

◆ **BACKGROUND BYTES:** The Bible was written in a part of the world where grapes, and therefore wine, were plentiful. Most of the biblical principles that apply to drugs and alcohol are found in the context of the Bible's views on wine and "hard drink."

◆ **SCRIPTURE BYTES:** While Jesus Himself turned water into wine for the sake of some guests at a wedding party (John 2:1-11), He is the "Living Water." He tells us that worshiping God in the Holy Spirit is the key to a fulfilling, full life (John 4:1-26; 10:10). Using a similar analogy we can note that Jesus, in one sense, is the "Ultimate High"—everything the "partyer" is looking for but will never find in drugs or alcohol. In that context, Paul's admonition to "be filled with the Holy Spirit, not wine" seems a quite contemporary message for today's teens (Ephesians 5:18).

SESSION ONE

STEP 4

The Ultimate High

Below, discuss insights about missing out on drugs and alcohol: 15-20 minutes. Or, choose one of the option categories highlighted in the left sidebar and see pages 25-29 for more "Getting the Point" options.

Supplies needed: copies of Resource 2, "Insight Cards," pens, newsprint, marker.
Set up: Ahead of time, cut out copies of Resource 2, "Insight Cards" (page 21).

Our culture does a great job portraying drug and alcohol use as something fun, relaxing, even sophisticated. But often, those promises are hollow. Only God can meet our needs that drugs and alcohol only temporarily cover up. Create a commercial that portrays your Bible passage and God's promise. It can be a dialogue between two friends or a catchy jingle. You decide!

After the students have presented their ads, have them stay in their groups. Ask volunteers to share what they wrote on their "Insight Cards" in Step 3. Use the newsprint and markers to make a list of their responses. Now refer back to the list of drug effects your students identified during Step 1.

Let's review. What are some "fun" reasons people use drugs and alcohol? Refer back to the Talkstarter.

How do these compare to the benefits of following God?

Conclude by saying something like: **Jesus is the Ultimate High. When we worship Him in the Holy Spirit, we experience to a fuller, more satisfying degree everything the "partyer" is looking for but will never really find in drugs or alcohol.**

OPTIONS

- EXTRA ACTION
- HEARD IT ALL BEFORE
- LITTLE BIBLE BACKGROUND
- FELLOWSHIP & WORSHIP
- MOSTLY GIRLS
- MOSTLY GUYS
- EXTRA FUN
- SHORT MEETING TIME
- URBAN

STEP 5

Customized Challenge

Below, students choose an appropriate challenge for them: 5 minutes. Or, choose one of the option categories highlighted in the right sidebar and see pages 25-29 for more "Getting Personal" options.

Supplies needed: index cards and pens.
Set up: Pass out index cards and pens.

Tell students to bow their heads and listen while you read this list of challenges. You don't have to use the exact challenges below. Customize the following to the needs you know your students have:

• **Are you using drugs and alcohol regularly? My challenge to you is to be honest with God. Admit your struggles to Him. If you're willing to change, tell Him that. Also, tell a trusted adult what you're going through. I'm willing to talk to you after the session.**

• **Is drug or alcohol use an off-and-on struggle for you— you wouldn't say you're a regular user, but sometimes you might have a beer or something at a party? My challenge to you is to get into an accountability relationship. Find a friend—maybe someone who has struggled in this area in the past but is doing better now—who can somehow show you what it means to be "filled with the Spirit." Commit to meeting with him or her by phone or in person for at least 15 minutes each week to share and pray for God's strength.**

• **Maybe you know in your head all the things we talked about today but you still *feel* like you're missing out on the fun. I challenge you to spend some time doing some fun things that are healthy for you. Make a list of all the things that you enjoy doing that don't involve drugs or alcohol. Then decide to do one or two this week. Thank God for the opportunity to enjoy yourself in a healthy way.**

• **Finally, if you're growing in the Lord and this is not an area of struggle for you, ask God to help you continue to yield your life to the work of his Holy Spirit. Pray that you will experience the real joy and power of God's "abundant" life.**

Ask students to choose a challenge and write it down on an index card. Encourage students to share what they wrote with at least one other person this week.

OPTIONS
- LARGE GROUP
- URBAN
- JR.HIGH/HIGH SCHOOL COMBINED
- EXTRA CHALLENGE

THE DRUG FREE CHALLENGE

Drugs and Alcohol Talkstarter

RESOURCE 1

1. **In your school, what percentage of the students do you think use drugs?**

    0%   10%   20%   30%   40%   50%   60%   70%   80%   90%   100%

    What percentage do you think drink alcohol?

    0%   10%   20%   30%   40%   50%   60%   70%   80%   90%   100%

2. **Why do you think so many students try drugs and alcohol?**
    - ___ They want to see what it feels like
    - ___ They think it's cool
    - ___ Their friends do it
    - ___ They want to get high
    - ___ They don't realize what they're doing
    - ___ They need something to help them cope with life
    - ___ They want to escape from reality
    - ___ Other:

3. **Which of the following statements do you agree with:**
    - ___ I believe drug and alcohol use, if done only once in a while, probably won't have an effect on you.
    - ___ I believe it's OK to drink socially (at a party or at dinner), as long as you don't get drunk.
    - ___ I believe that drug and alcohol use is usually a symptom of deeper issues.
    - ___ I believe that you can't have a social life if you don't go to parties where drugs and alcohol are being served.
    - ___ I believe that any use of illegal drugs or getting drunk is a sin.
    - ___ I could hide drug and alcohol use from my parents.

4. **Which of the following drugs do you think are OK for a teenager to try?**
    - ___ Tobacco (nicotine)
    - ___ Heroin
    - ___ Aspirin
    - ___ Model-airplane glue
    - ___ Marijuana
    - ___ Coffee (caffeine)
    - ___ Alcohol
    - ___ Anabolic steroids
    - ___ Methamephetamines
    - ___ Cocaine
    - ___ Other:
    - ___ None of the above

Adapted from the "Drugs Talkstarter" and "Alcohol Talkstarter" in the *One Kid at a Time Mentor Handbook* by Miles McPherson with Wayne Rice (Cook Ministry Resources). Used by permission.

THE DRUG FREE CHALLENGE

RESOURCE 2

Insight Cards

When I consider the "benefits" of following God, I think:

When I consider the "benefits" of following God, I think:

When I consider the "benefits" of following God, I think:

When I consider the "benefits" of following God, I think:

When I consider the "benefits" of following God, I think:

When I consider the "benefits" of following God, I think:

THE DRUG FREE CHALLENGE

optional RESOURCE 3

Left Out

Stuck home, Friday night . . . that's OK . . . I'll make the best of it.

See, it's just me and God, and I got my Bible here. What could be more fun than this, right? (Sits down to read his Bible.)

(Standing up abruptly.) Fun . . . Fun? Who am I kidding?

I should've gone to that party. That's the life right? All the rest of the guys, they're not worried about their bodies—they don't miss a few little brain cells. They're certainly not concerned about what God has to say.

(Pretending he's at the party) Hey, everybody, the life of the party's here! Check me out! (Pretends to guzzle a beer.) That's my second beer. C'mon, give me another one. I'm starting to get a buzz.

(Not pretending anymore) I know, I know. That could never really make me happy. How could I feel good about my relationship with God the morning after I partied? What would I tell my Christian friends?

But that's what gets me so mad sometimes, God! I can't win! It seems like the people who don't know You get to have all the fun! It doesn't seem fair.

Sometimes I think You just want me to live a boring life.

(Sitting back down, grabbing the Bible.) I'll just sit here with my halo on. I'll play the angel.

Stuck here on a Friday night. I got my Bible right here. I don't need anything else . . . right?

MEDIA

THE DRUG FREE CHALLENGE

optional RESOURCE 4

Dear Abbey

Dear Abbey,
I've been invited to a party where I know people will be drinking beer. A lot of my friends will be there. I don't want to drink but I like hanging out with everybody. Should I go to the party if I don't drink anything? Or should I just avoid the temptation altogether?
Signed,
PARTY POOPER

Dear Party Pooper,
I tell my students that "a plane takes off best against the wind." What do I mean by this? Two things. First, Jesus was right in the thick of things all the time. I try to teach my kids that they need to be actively involved in witnessing to their friends in real, authentic ways. This might mean that they go to the parties because that's where kids are. Also, I believe that kids who are at these parties and intoxicated and drugged up are at their most vulnerable. And I don't mean that this is an opportunity to manipulate them; rather I believe that these kids have a clearer glimpse of who they really are. And this glimpse shows them that they are miserable, hurting, lonely, depressed, and so on. When a Christian teen befriends this kid at a party in a loving, non-condemning way, the opportunity of true witnessing can occur.

Dear Abbey,
When I'm offered a can of beer or a drag on a cigarette, what can I say that won't make me sound like a loser?
Signed,
CLOSET JESUS FAN

Dear Closet Jesus Fan,
This question needs to be addressed, handled, and answered WAY before you actually get asked the question. I believe boundaries need to be firmly decided upon and drawn in a person's life. It's healthy and I know kids want and appreciate such.

Dear Abbey,
It's not always easy to stay focused on my walk with God. When I'm at church or at home, it's easier. But when I'm around my friends who party, God seems to slip my mind. What can I do?
Signed,
BACKSLIDER

Dear Backslider,
Be spiritually prepared. Read the Word, pray, attend Bible study and church. Two, have a partner. Someone who's is praying for you, edifying you and is going to ask the hard questions. Three, forewarned is forearmed. Know the enemy and know what you're up against. Tempting situations are going to happen, but don't be caught off guard.

Dear Abbey,
I've never had a drink of alcohol in my life. I've never smoked a cigarette. I've never tried any narcotic drugs. And I have a reputation around school of being a "goodie-goodie." I hate that. I'm trying to make smart decisions and I get labeled like that. What can I do about it?
Signed,
GOODIE 2 SHOES

Dear Goody 2 Shoes,
Laugh. Understand the big picture. You've got something other people don't. Remember and believe that you are called by God to a higher purpose and a higher calling.

OPTIONS

SESSION ONE

EXTRA ACTION

STEP 1 - SURVIVAL TEAMS
Teams of five try to overcome handicaps and enemy bombs to make it to the end.

Split your group into five-person survival teams. Tell the teams that their goal is to get their entire team to the "drug-free zone" within a certain time limit. The drug-free zone (an outside location) should be a good distance away from the initial meeting location. The problem is that certain members of their team are handicapped. One is deaf (give them earphones), two are blind (blindfolded), one is unconscious (require him or her to be motionless throughout the activity), and only one member is completely healthy. Tell groups they will receive one million dollars for each team member that makes it to the drug-free zone under the time limit (12 minutes). While teams attempt this dangerous mission, make life more difficult for them by pelting them with enemy "bombs" (soft playground balls or paper wads, for example). Discuss: **Did you ever feel like leaving someone behind? Why was it important to work as a team and not leave anyone behind?** *(Needed: blindfolds, playground balls.)*

STEP 4 - TOSS UP
Toss balls and share thoughts.

Ahead of time, label three tennis balls "thought," "feeling," and "counsel." Have students stand in a circle and toss the balls in a repeating pattern. Randomly call out "stop." The three students who are holding balls at that time must should shout either a thought or feeling about drugs or alcohol use, or counsel that they might give to someone contemplating using drugs. Encourage students on their turn to share some thoughts and feelings they wrote on their Insight Cards in Step 3. *(Needed: three tennis balls.)*

SMALL GROUP

STEP 1 - WHERE'S MINE?
Leave some students feeling left out when you pass out cookies.

Start your group by telling students you have some extra cookies (or other favorite food or candy) in your office that you would like to share with them. As you pass out the treats, take one yourself, and give some to the other students, but run out while several students are left empty-handed. Vaguely apologize for not having enough, then continue to enjoy your goodies. Keep the gag going as long as you're comfortable with it, but finally break out extra cookies and explain you were trying to make a point. Talk about how food can be similar to people and their quest for drugs or alcohol. Ask your students how they felt when they either received or didn't receive a cookie. *(Needed: cookies.)*

STEP 3 - MUST SEE TV
Videotape TV ads showing what the Christian life has to offer.

Ahead of time, record commercials or get clippings from magazines that glorify drug and alcohol use. As you display and discuss what the ads communicate to people, say: **We are now going to make our own commercial advertising how God can help with everyday struggles.** With a camcorder and a TV hookup you can now have fun making your own ad. Assign volunteers to play roles on the commercial crew (parts will depend on size of your small group). Give your group a few minutes to brainstorm and then video the live commercial based on the verses studied in Step 3. Of course you will have some laughter and mess ups, but this will only add to the fun! After you have completed the video get your students looking forward to next week by saying you will be debuting the edited version of the new commercial. *(Needed: TV, VCR, camcorder.)*

LARGE GROUP

STEP 2 - SOOOO COMMERCIAL
Give three students a chance to make impromptu commercials for drugs.

Ask for three volunteers to come up front. Give one person an empty beer can, another a pack of unopened cigarettes, and the third a bottle of pills (aspirin—just for effect). Say: **Okay, we know the media paints a picture of drinking and smoking as something sophisticated, cool, and mature. Our three volunteers are going to have one minute to try to be as persuasive as possible as they "sell" you on the benefits of their product. At the end, you will decide who did the best job by an "applause meter."** Encourage volunteers to do a quick skit off the top of their heads. Give a prize to the student who receives the loudest applause. Use the discussion questions at the end of Step 2. *(Needed: empty beer can, unopened cigarettes, empty bottle of pills.)*

STEP 5 - BREAK DOWN
Break down into small groups to discuss which challenge students will accept.

Many large groups have small group programs. If you don't have one yet, you might consider investigating what it would take to start one. Present the challenge as directed in Step 5. Then break down into small groups; ideally there will be one adult leader in each group of six to eight students. Students can share with their group what challenge they are targeting for their own life. This does two things. 1) It facilitates accountability—no student should have to walk through the tough issues surrounding drugs and alcohol without being able to tell others what's going on. 2) It may prevent some struggling students from slipping through the cracks.

OPTIONS

SESSION ONE

HEARD IT ALL BEFORE

STEP 2 - THE OTHER SIDE
Students make print or "live action" ads showing the down sides of drug use.

Tape three or four current TV beer ads that most students will be familiar with, or cut print ads from magazines or newspapers. (You might also collect cigarette ads.) Evaluate whether the ads depict the true picture of alcohol or tobacco use or glorify it. Discuss: **How does this ad say your life will change if you smoke these cigarettes or drink this brand of alcohol?** Then have students create and perform a roleplay showing the devastating "down sides" of alcohol or drug abuse. Prompt them to depict scenes of violence, family brokenness, lost opportunities, alcohol- related accidents, and so on all of which are clearly associated with substance abuse. Students can present their findings as a "freeze frame" or "live action." *(Needed: tape, magazine ads.)*

STEP 4 - PAT VS. ABBEY
Roleplay situations that involve getting the same "pat" answers.

Divide students into groups of three. In each group, tell the student with the biggest Bible he or she gets to be "Pat." Of the two left, the one with more hair gets to be "Christian" and the remaining person gets to play "Abbey." Take a look at the optional Resource 4, "Dear Abbey" (page 24). Instead of using this as written, use the letters as examples of scenarios Christian could roleplay, for example, Christian could play someone who is tired of being called a "goodie, goodie." Pat should answer Christian's questions with, you guessed it, "pat" answers—your church kids will know them all well. Abbey should give an answer that is not pat and predictable. Ask Christian what it felt like to get these answers to his or her deep dilemmas. *(Needed: Resource 4.)*

LITTLE BIBLE BACKGROUND

STEP 3 - MORE BENEFITS
Discuss more benefits of following God.

If you think your group is interested in more of the benefits God bestows on Christians, try this. Give each small group a portion of Ephesians 1:1—3:21. Read Ephesians 1:3 aloud, telling students that the book of Ephesians lists a couple dozen blessings (benefits) that are showered on Christians. For example, 1:4 says that God chose us before the creation of the world. The next verse says He has adopted us into His family. Have your groups search their portions and list or underline as many blessings as they can find. Then, list their results on a chalkboard or newsprint and discuss the meaning of each blessing; or go ahead with the original suggestion to make creative presentations of the findings featuring bumper stickers, jingles, or a talk show dialogue. Be sure to point out just how incredibly fortunate we are to have a God who gives us so much. *(Needed: chalkboard and chalk, or newsprint and pens.)*

STEP 4 - WHAT DO YOU THINK?
Students share a response to hypothetical questions.

For best results, sit in a circle. Take a look at the optional Resource 4, "Dear Abbey" (page 24). Instead of using this as written (for example, as a series of "Dear Abbey" letters), use just the letters as examples of questions students ask about drugs and alcohol. Read aloud the letters hypothetical teens wrote in to "Abbey." Tell students to take turns sharing their responses to the question. If you want, compare students' answers included on the resource. *(Needed: Resource 4.)*

FELLOWSHIP & WORSHIP

STEP 2 - DRUG COLLAGES
Make collages including pictures that glorify drug and alcohol use.

Encourage students to get into groups of three or four with people they don't know very well. Say: **Advertising and the media do a great job depicting the positive aspects of a lifestyle that include drugs and alcohol. People who drink are often portrayed as sophisticated, fun-loving, relaxed, and mature. Take the next five to seven minutes and put together a collage of ads, pictures, and words that would convince someone of the benefits of alcohol/drug use.** Pass out collage supplies. Let each group make a collage as directed. If time permits, have a spokesperson from each group share a persuasive presentation about the benefits of a lifestyle that includes drugs/alcohol according to their collage. *(Needed: a stack of newspapers and magazines which include a number of advertisements for alcoholic beverages and cigarettes, especially those which emphasize lifestyle, a large piece of posterboard, a couple of glue sticks, scissors, and a thick marker.)*

STEP 4 - ULTIMATE PARTY
Worship and celebrate Jesus as the Ultimate High.

Worship, at its best, is like a party where all the participants get drunk on the Holy Spirit. One of the best ways to help students who feel like they're "missing out" on the fun of drugs and alcohol, is to teach them how to worship well. Sing songs that celebrate following Jesus. Let students share how grateful they are for Jesus in their own words. Share reflective thoughts about what Jesus means to you. Do what you can to create a festive atmosphere.

OPTIONS

SESSION ONE

MOSTLY GIRLS

STEP 1 - PARTY ALTERNATIVE
Have girls brainstorm fun ideas that are alternatives to drug and alcohol parties.

Have the girls brainstorm fun ideas that are alternatives to the parties where chemicals are involved. Get girls brainstorming right away. For example, make your own pizza at the local pizza joint. Build a mega-sundae. Rent a stupid but fun video and have people come dressed as their favorite character. Discuss: **You've probably heard people say before that parties are more fun when there's drugs and alcohol available. It seems like people think drugs and alcohol make everything more fun! What do you think? Can you have just as much or maybe more fun without using drugs or alcohol?**

STEP 4 - DEAR ABBEY
Use the "Dear Abbey" resource to discuss frequently asked questions.

Before passing out copies of the optional Resource 4, "Dear Abbey" (page 24), read the letters (not "Abbey's" response), and ask students what advice they might give, if they were responding to the letters. Then pass out copies of the resource and discuss what students think of Abbey's answers. *(Needed: copies of Resource 4.)*

MOSTLY GUYS

STEP 1 - REMEMBER WHEN . . .
Guys remember the gross, stupid, and loud highlights of the previous year.

Guys love to remember the gross, the loud, the stupid, or awesome prank they pulled on someone. Give your guys just a few minutes and ask them to share the gross, loud, stupid, and funny highlights of their previous year. Give a can of something gross (like Spam) or some stupid prize to the guy who tells the best story. Your transition to the lesson could go something like this: **I obviously missed out on some of the nasty and smelly stuff you guys did recently. It sounds like a lot of fun. Would your friends think this was fun? What would other people consider more fun?**

STEP 4 - FITNESS PLANS
Guys make plans to be both fun and fit.

Step 4 starts off by comparing the way athletes separate their bodies and minds for their physical goals with the way Christians should separate their minds, bodies, and spirits for their goal to live for God. This is an idea guys can really relate to. Expand on this idea. Ask guys who participate on sports teams to share what past or present sacrifices they have made or are making due to their training. Pass out pens and paper. Ask students to list things that they need to separate themselves from to live for God. Then have them list all the things they can think of to do in "training" for God that will help them both have fun and be spiritually "fit."

EXTRA FUN

STEP 1 - RUSSIAN ROULETTE
Egg, cream, or pie-in-the-face one out of every six students.

Most kids are aware that just messing around with drugs doesn't guarantee that you will become a hopeless addict. Because they are kids, they feel invincible and live by the motto "It'll never happen to me." You can bring to light the idea that using drugs is a crap shoot with your life—"Russian roulette" with little to gain and much to lose. Discuss: **Out of all the teens who experiment with drugs, how many do you think will have no serious consequences? How many do you think will get seriously messed up? How do you know who will get messed up and who won't?** (No one can know.) Have students take turns rolling one die. Congratulate each student that rolls a six—they have just become one of the lucky ones who get "messed up" by drugs. To symbolize this, "mess them up" with shaving cream, an egg, or a pie in the face. Tell students "1 in 6" is a number you pulled out of your hat—there's no hard evidence to support it. But the point is: **Why would you want to take that chance?** *(Needed: eggs, shaving cream, or pies.)*

STEP 4 - OIL AND WATER
Give students a fun, concrete way to remember drugs and Christians don't mix.

Some things are not compatible. A mind controlled by the Holy Spirit and a mind controlled by drugs are like oil and water. You can't mix them together. A person makes a choice when they stand at the crossroads of drug use: to have God control their minds or allow their minds to be controlled by a substance. Have some fun illustrating this by using a cup of cooking oil and a cup of water (use a bit of food coloring to brighten it up). Dump both into an empty glass jar. Stir it, shake it, and the two still separate. Christians and chemicals are not compatible.

OPTIONS

SESSION ONE

MEDIA

STEP 1 - CANDID CAMERA
Interview "typical teens" about drugs.

Take your video camera to a mall or teen hangout and interview as many teens as you can—or better yet, coach some of your students to do the interviews. Ask teens if you can interview them, be honest and upfront about what you're doing, and thank them for helping. Try to get 5-10 minutes of tape time from a wide variety of students. Use questions like: **How common is drug use at your school? What drugs have you used? What drugs do you think are OK for teens to use? Are there any drugs you should never take? Why? Do you think whether or not you believe in God should affect whether or not you take drugs or drink alcohol?** After the video, discuss what your students think of the answers given. *(Needed: video camera, videotape, TV, VCR.)*

STEP 2 - VIDEO MONOLOGUE
Videotape an actor reading Resource 3.

On the optional Resource 3, "Left Out" page 23, a typical Christian teen is stuck home on a Friday night and feeling "left out." Prepare an actor to perform this monologue in front of the camera. The video will automatically engage students and keep away the giggles and heckling.
TIP: The following tip is effective not just for the monologue above, but for any time you film interviews. Think in terms of three cameras. Any time you can, between questions and comments, stop and move to a new position. Although you have only one camera, it will seem like you have more.

SHORT MEETING TIME

STEP 2 - ACTIVE DISCUSSION
Discuss talkstarter questions as a group.

Instead of breaking into small groups, use Resource 1 as a guide for your discussion and let students answer with their bodies. For questions 1 and 2, set up a spectrum in your room—point to one end of the room and call it "100%" and call the other end "0%"; tell the students to answer in terms of a percentage of students by where they stand in the room. For questions 3 and 4, have students stand up when they agree with a statement and sit down for when they disagree. *(Needed: copy of Resource 1.)*

STEP 3/4 - INSIGHT CARDS
Skip the presentations.

Instead of introducing the "Insight Cards" (Resource 2) at the end of Step 3, use this resource to help focus and streamline the entire step. Instead of reading Scripture and then making a creative presentation, simply give students a few minutes to read all the Scripture on their own and write down their "insights" as directed in Step 3. This activity will lead more fluidly into Step 4. *(Needed: Resource 2, pens or pencils.)*

URBAN

STEP 4 - ADDICTS' HIGH
Design a high school for drug addicts

Keep students in the groups they did their Bible studies in and announce that they are now to pretend that they are a council of urban Christian educators about to embark upon starting a Christian high school which will be an area-wide magnet school for drug abusers (believers and new converts). By using one of the Scriptures which was given during the earlier activity each group will do the following: 1) Name the Christian high school; 2) Define which two drugs addictions the school will focus on; 3) Create a motto for the school from Scripture; 4) Design a curriculum of eight classes (two per year) which will help the addict and heal his or her soul. Give students a few minutes to brainstorm, then have each group describe the school they designed to the entire group.

STEP 5 - HOLY GHOST PARTY
Celebrate the ministry of the Holy Spirit.

As a festive closer, have what R&B gospel musician Kirk Franklin calls "A Holy Ghost Party!" This can be a small or big party and can be at the end or take the majority of your meeting time. Include light food and snacks, Christian music, and some games. The purpose is to celebrate the power of God's Spirit (our Comforter) who helps us overcome all addictions (physical and moral) even though there are tough episodes. Finally, a "Holy Ghost Party" must include at some point a reading and reflection of Acts 2 which describes the first experience with the Holy Spirit at Pentecost. Be sure to reflect that the persons at the first celebration had real problems and addictions in their lives, but that it was the power of the Spirit at Pentecost who gave them victory over sin through Jesus Christ our Lord.

OPTIONS

SESSION ONE

STEP 2 - RING AROUND THE CAN
Play a sort of four-way tug-o'-war game.

Play with four students at a time (all girls or all boys). Have contestants circle up and each grab one end of two pieces of rope so that the rope connects all four of them in a circle. Contestants are eliminated if they touch the trash can or let go of the rope. Keep eliminating girls until only one is left. Repeat the same process with the guys. Afterwards, lead a discussion comparing the circles formed with the ropes with circles of friendship you experience. Both are difficult, and at times students get eliminated from the circle. Ask: **What kinds of things are we eliminated from because we're Christians? Why do we eliminate ourselves from drug and alcohol use? What are the advantages?**

STEP 5 - POSITIVE PEER PRESSURE
Use accountability and prayer to encourage each other.

Instead of praying as a group, capitalize on the peer pressure that both junior and senior highers face through the positive peer pressure of prayer and accountability. Break into groups by school. This provides more natural opportunities for accountability, as well as potential similarity of temptations (for example, the new temptations of junior high school or the big school Friday night football party). Within their school groups, ask students to partner off to pray for each other and encourage them to serve as positive peer pressure for each other when they see each other at school or extracurricular events. If someone is the only student from a certain school, pair him or her with an adult leader or with another student who is also the sole student from their school.

STEP 3 - SEPARATED
Study how God separated Matthew from his old life for God's purposes.

Read the story of Matthew in Mark 2:13-17, Matthew 9:9-13, and Luke 5:27-32. Make two columns on newsprint and have students shout out to you things Matthew stopped doing when he converted and began to commit himself to following Jesus. Next have students shout out to you things that Matthew started doing—the things that Jesus was doing in His life for example. The most obvious example is the incredible opportunity Matthew had to follow and learn from Jesus. Compare the two lists. **For Matthew, the price of giving up his old way of life for God's purposes was well worth it because he had a higher purpose for his life than just doing what he wanted for his own gain. Matthew knew that his love relationship with Jesus would never end—it would lead to eternity in heaven. If we trust Jesus for our sins we can be assured of the same thing.**

STEP 5 - FRUIT CARDS
Send encouraging letters to others.

Bring in some cards with blank insides. For best results, use cards with fruit on the front. Using Galatians 5:22-25 as a guide, help students identify which of the fruits of the Spirit seem to be most lacking in their lives. Tell them to, as a seed of faith, write a "fruit card" to someone else. For example, if they are in need of peace, they might send a card to someone blessing them with the peace of God. You and your students may be surprised at the results.

STEP 1 (5-10 MIN. UNLESS NOTED)
- ❑ **Extra Action:** Survival Teams
- ❑ **Small Group:** Where's Mine?
- ❑ **Mostly Girls:** Party Alternative (15+ min.)
- ❑ **Mostly Guys:** Remember When . . .
- ❑ **Extra Fun:** Russian Roulette
- ❑ **Media:** Candid Camera

STEP 2 (10-15 MIN. UNLESS NOTED)
- ❑ **Large Group:** Soooo Commercial
- ❑ **Heard It All:** The Other Side
- ❑ **Fellowship & Worship:** Drug Collages
- ❑ **Media:** Video Monologue
- ❑ **Short Time:** Active Discussion (5-10 min.)
- ❑ **Combined:** Ring Around the Can

STEP 3 (15-20 MIN. UNLESS NOTED)
- ❑ **Small Group:** Must See TV
- ❑ **Little Bible:** More Benefits
- ❑ **Short Time:** Insight Cards (10-15 min.)*
- ❑ **Extra Challenge:** Separated

STEP 4 (10-15 MIN. UNLESS NOTED)
- ❑ **Extra Action:** Toss Up
- ❑ **Heard It All:** Pat vs. Abbey
- ❑ **Little Bible:** What Do You Think?
- ❑ **Fellowship & Worship:** Ultimate Party
- ❑ **Mostly Girls:** Dear Abbey
- ❑ **Mostly Guys:** Fitness Plans
- ❑ **Extra Fun:** Oil and Water
- ❑ **Urban:** Addicts' High

STEP 5 (5-10 MIN. UNLESS NOTED)
- ❑ **Large Group:** Break Down
- ❑ **Urban:** Holy Ghost Party
- ❑ **Combined:** Positive Peer Pressure
- ❑ **Extra Challenge:** Fruit Cards

* combined steps

SESSION 2
Coping With Life in a Cop-Out Culture

YOUR GOALS FOR THIS SESSION:
Choose one or more

☐ To help students learn that using drugs and alcohol is copping out, not coping—it only leads to more problems.

☐ To help students understand that Jesus can give them the power to cope with life's struggles.

☐ To equip students with healthy coping strategies, such as spending time in God's Word, praying, and leaning on the support of Christian friends.

☐ Other: _____

Your Bible Base:

Hebrews 4:15-16
Philippians 4:6-7
James 1:2-5

SESSION TWO

STEP 1

Don't Get Buzzed

Below, teams compete in a variation of the party game "Taboo": 5-10 minutes. Or, choose an option category from the right sidebar and see pages 41-45 for more "Getting the Point" options.

Supplies needed: cut-up copy of Resource 5, "Coping Cards" (page 37), timer, buzzer or bell.
Set up: Cut up one copy of Resource 5 and put the cards in a bag. Divide into two teams and tell teams to choose one clue-giver.

Have the first team's clue-giver choose a card from the bag. Once he or she silently reads the "clue word" and the "off-limit list," he or she must hand you the card. Start the timer and give the clue-giver 30 seconds to get his or her team to name the clue word. The clue-giver can use any combination of words, phrases, and sentences to give his or her team clues except for any of the words—or any form of the words—on the off-limit list. If the clue-giver says anything illegal or goes over the time limit, "buzz" him or her out with your buzzer or bell. Rotate clue-givers until all the cards are used. Award one point for each correct answer and congratulate the winning team.

Did you catch what all of the clue words had in common? (Each clue word names a "coping mechanism," or a way of dealing with life's problems.)

Remind students what all nine coping mechanisms were. **Which of these coping mechanisms do you think are most popular among people your age? Why? Which of these do you think are the least popular ways of dealing with problems? Why?**

Besides the ways mentioned on these cards, what other ways do people try to cope with their problems?

Turn to the person next to you and share two ways you typically cope with your problems.

OPTIONS

- EXTRA ACTION
- LARGE GROUP
- LITTLE BIBLE BACKGROUND
- MOSTLY GIRLS
- MOSTLY GUYS
- EXTRA FUN
- SHORT MEETING TIME
- URBAN

STEP 2

Coping Quotes

Below, students discuss five quotes about drug and alcohol use, then read a true story about where one teen's choices led: 10-15 minutes.
Or, choose an option category highlighted in the left sidebar and see pages 41-45 for more "Getting Thirsty" options.

Supplies needed: copies of Resource 6, "Coping Quotes" (page 38), and Resource 7, "Choices" (page 39).
Set up: For best results, sit in a circle. Pass out copies of Resource 6.

Resource 6 has a slightly different format than the talkstarter used in Session 1. It will cause students to think a little more about what they want to say. But you want to establish the same discussion guidelines. Establish an atmosphere where every student knows his or her opinion is valued. Read each quote about drug and alcohol use one at a time. Then have students share either a thought, feeling, or Bible verse that applies to the quote.

What's the difference between coping and copping out?
Copping out is running away from or burying your problems. Coping with your problems means not being afraid of pain when life is painful. It's sticking it out. It's facing life head on, even when that's not the easiest thing to do. Why do you think so many people have a hard time coping with life?

Do you think most people who depend on drugs just decide one day, "Hey, I think I'll get addicted to alcohol or strung out on drugs because I don't know any better way to deal with life"? What do you think happens instead?

To help students process this question, pass out the case study on Resource 7. Read this true story about Reed aloud and discuss: **Reed had a tough family background. Do you think he did a good job coping with his problems or did he cop out? Why?**

What are some things Reed could have done to help him cope with his problems in healthy ways?

SESSION TWO

STEP 3

A Better Way to Cope

Below, students study three promises from God to help them cope: 15-20 minutes. Or, choose an option category from the right sidebar and see pages 41-45 for more "Getting the Word" options.

Supplies needed: Bibles.
Set up: Divide into three groups and assign each group one of these three passages: Hebrews 4:15-16; Philippians 4:6-7; or James 1:2-5.

Each of the three passages contains a type of "problem" we all face, along with a promise from God in response to that problem. You might introduce this study by saying something like: **If we don't use drugs and alcohol to cope with life, what should we do? Let's see what the Bible has to say.** Give groups a few minutes to list the problem addressed and the promise God gives to help us cope with the problem. Have each group appoint a spokesperson to share their group's answers. Encourage students to take notes on the other presentations.

Here are some possible answers for you to guide your students toward:

- **Group 1: Hebrews 4:15-16**
  The Problem: Temptations; any time of need.
  The Promise: We will receive mercy and find grace to help in our time of need.

- **Group 2: Philippians 4:6-7**
  The Problem: Things that cause us to worry or become anxious.
  The Promise: God's peace will guard our hearts and minds in Christ Jesus.

- **Group 3: James 1:2-5**
  The Problem: Trials of many kinds.
  The Promise: Trials make us mature and complete. If we do not understand the purpose of our trials, we are to ask God and He will give us understanding.

At this time, summarize the difference between relying on God's promises to cope with life and relying on drugs and alcohol. For example, you might say: **God is not a drug. He doesn't promise to dull our pain. He's not an escape from tough times. He simply promises to walk with us through our struggles. The**

OPTIONS

SMALL GROUP

LARGE GROUP

HEARD IT ALL BEFORE

MOSTLY GUYS

EXTRA CHALLENGE

Bible is very upfront about the fact that life is tough. Tough times happen. The Bible also tells us that, as Christians, we don't have to turn to drugs or alcohol or anything else to help us cope when life gets tough. God is enough. God can help us get through our problems.

> ## Jesus' example
> *Matthew 26:36-46—Jesus in the Garden of Gethsemane*
>
> - ◆ **BACKGROUND BYTES:** The Garden of Gethsemane was an important place where Jesus often went to pray. The night Jesus was betrayed He spoke with His Father about the trying times ahead. Jesus poured out His heart to God as He confronted the bloody events He knew would come. • The "cup" Jesus referred to in His prayer represented suffering and death.
> - ◆ **SCRIPTURE BYTES:** The way Jesus prayed to God was more relational and familiar than any Jew in that day would have prayed. Jesus stressed His relationship with the Father. For other places where Jesus prays to God in a tough situation, see: Luke 5:10-1; Mark 6:15-39. • Jesus not only modeled leaning on God in prayer, He also gave us the promise that He would help us in our times of need, through the Holy Spirit. See: James 17:1-7; 1 Corinthians 16:11; and Hebrews 4:12-20.
> - ◆ **BYTE-SIZE INSIGHTS:** If life was painful for Jesus while He lived on earth, we can be certain it will be painful for us. God didn't take away Jesus' pain. But Jesus knew that prayer to God was the one place He could go to get comfort and help to deal with His pain. Praying to God didn't make Jesus' pain go away. It didn't even numb the pain. It did give Jesus the courage to cope with His struggles. Copping out is dulling the pain. Jesus showed us how to cope with life.

SESSION TWO

STEP 4

The PRAY Strategy

Below, students rotate to different "stations" where they discuss the PRAY strategy for coping with life: 15-20 minutes.
Or, choose an option category highlighted in the right sidebar and see pages 41-45 for more "Getting Personal" and "Getting the Point" options.

Supplies needed: leather strings, beads with the letters P, R, A, and Y on them (optional).
Set up: You need four station leaders who are adults or mature students. Choose leaders who can lead their station by example. Use the directions below to prepare your leaders ahead of time. Designate four areas in your room as your "stations."

Small groups should rotate and spend about 5-7 minutes at each station. At each station the leader should: 1) talk briefly to define his or her station and give details about how he or she uses the particular strategy to cope with life, and 2) use the discussion questions below to facilitate a practical follow-up discussion.

Optional: Prepare each leader with enough beads for each student. The beads should say the letter of each station on them. At the end of rotating through the stations, pass out leather strings. Help students put their beads together to make bracelets that remind them to PRAY.

STATION 1: PRAYER—Prayer is an effective coping mechanism when we understand that God wants us to express our real, honest emotions about our struggles. Prepare the station leader to share in detail how he or she talks to God with honesty and emotion.

Discuss: **Does prayer help you cope with your problems? Why or why not? Do you have any questions about prayer in general? Do you have any questions about how to be honest with God about your emotions and struggles?**

STATION 2: READING THE BIBLE—Reading the Bible is an effective coping mechanism when we bring an open heart and listen to what God has to say to us. Prepare the station leader to share in detail how he or she listens to God through Scripture reading.

Discuss: **Does reading the Bible help you cope with your problems? Why or why not? Do you have any questions about reading the Bible in general? Do you have any questions about how to hear what God wants you to hear when you study the Bible?**

OPTIONS

- EXTRA ACTION
- SMALL GROUP
- HEARD IT ALL BEFORE
- LITTLE BIBLE BACKGROUND
- FELLOWSHIP & WORSHIP
- MOSTLY GIRLS
- EXTRA FUN
- MEDIA
- SHORT MEETING TIME
- URBAN
- JR. HIGH/HIGH SCHOOL COMBINED
- EXTRA CHALLENGE

35

STATION 3: ACCOUNTABILITY—Building accountability friendships involves getting together with friends who are also committed to God and keeping one another on track. Prepare the station leader to share in detail how his or her own accountability friendships help him or her cope with tough times.

Discuss: **Do your friends help you cope with your problems? Why or why not? Do you have any questions about accountability friendships in general? Do you have any questions about how to build the kind of accountability friendships that will support you and help you cope?**

STATION 4: YOUTH GROUP—Committing to the youth group is an effective coping mechanism because God can use the group to provide support, encouragement, and spiritual direction. Prepare the station leader to share in detail how his or her own youth group provided these benefits.

Discuss: **Does the youth group help you cope with your problems? Why or why not? Do you have any questions about how you might take some steps towards the youth group so that the youth group might help you cope with your struggles?**

Bring the group back together. Summarize the lesson. For example, you might say something like: **Maybe drugs and alcohol are a real temptation for you. Or maybe anger, denial, busyness, or depression are more common in your life. Whatever unhealthy coping devices you may use, recognize that they are walls that keep you from experiencing the real peace and faith that God promises. When life gets tough, please remember to PRAY. Put that strategy into action by praying, reading the Bible, building accountability friendships, and committing to the youth group.** Close in prayer, thanking God for His help in our times of struggle.

THE DRUG FREE CHALLENGE

RESOURCE 5

Coping Cards

SMOKING CIGARETTES

OFF-LIMIT LIST:
smoke, cigarettes, nicotine, tobacco, drag

PROCRASTINATING

OFF-LIMIT LIST:
procrastinate, put off, avoid, wait

USING ALCOHOL

OFF-LIMIT LIST:
alcohol, drinking, partying, beer, bottle

WORRYING

OFF-LIMIT LIST:
worry, stress, anxiety, panic, fret

OVEREATING

OFF-LIMIT LIST:
eat, food, pig out, stuffed, a lot

GET BUSY

OFF-LIMIT LIST:
busy, action, do, work, hurry

SPACING OUT

OFF-LIMIT LIST:
space, veg, daydream, nothing, sit

PITY PARTY

OFF-LIMIT LIST:
pity, sympathy, sorry, depressed, beat up

THE DRUG FREE CHALLENGE
Coping Quotes

RESOURCE 6

1. Share a thought, feeling, or verse...
"Most teens who use drugs and alcohol are just immature and insecure. Drugs are their way to escape the pressures of adolescence."

2. Share a thought, feeling, or verse...
"My life stinks! I drink a lot because drinking helps me get through life. When I'm drinking, I don't have to think about all my problems."

3. Share a thought, feeling, or verse...
"Everybody needs something to get through life. Some people overeat. Some people have to complain to everybody about every little thing. My thing is I use cocaine. It's no big deal. I'm no worse than the guy who's addicted to watching TV. It's what I use to get through life, one day at a time."

4. Share a thought, feeling, or verse...
"If my parents knew that I was smoking weed, they'd be ticked. But they're hypocrites. They smoked when they were my age—in fact, they did a lot worse things than I did! I've got my whole life to be serious. I just want to have a good time while I'm young. What's wrong with that?"

5. Share a thought, feeling, or verse...
"I haven't had a job in two years. I'm living out of a paper box these days. If I can bum some loose change off a yuppie downtown tonight, I'm gonna go get me some more crack as fast as I can. I need my high so bad right now I'm shaking. If anyone tells you drugs help you cope with life, tell him he's a dope."

THE DRUG FREE CHALLENGE

RESOURCE 7

CASE STUDY: CHOICES

Reed didn't come from a "**CHURCHED**" background. **He was a skater,** and somewhat of a rebel—*often in trouble at school and at home.* When he moved from San Antonio to Colorado, he started attending the small youth group I led. He sometimes caused more than his share of trouble there, too, but he was a **GENUINE "SEEKER."** He was interested in spiritual things; he wanted to find out what God had to offer him. After a few short months, Reed gave his life to Christ. His life began to change for the better. His **parents, teachers,** and **friends** all noticed a difference in him. During an inner city mission trip with his youth group that summer, Reed hit the HIGH POINT of his spiritual life. Not only was he himself experiencing a new relationship with God, but *he began to tell others about what God could do for them.* His was the kind of story that makes youth workers love their job. Who would have thought that less than a year later, Reed, of all people, would be on the street, his life falling apart because of his addiction to drugs. **HOW DID REED GET FROM SUCH A SPIRITUAL HIGH TO THE ULTIMATE LOW?** Did he wake up one day and decide to throw his life away by becoming a hopeless addict? Of course not. It doesn't happen that way in the real world. In the real world, one choice leads to another and, well, here's how it went for Reed . . .

As we returned home, within the next couple of months, **Reed's family began to have problems.** They stoped going to church, considered divorce, and argued all the time. During this time, Reed began to experience problems with grades, teachers, and other authority figures. Over the next several months, Reed began to **slowly** and **inconspicuously** *withdraw from his friends and his youth group.*

Reed couldn't stand to be around his house and could not get along with his parents. He started hanging out with new friends, friends who seemed more "**REAL**" and who seemed to be able to relate to what he was going through. Reed's new friends did drugs and Reed started using soon after. Reed did not choose the friends because of their habits, he adopted their habits because they became his friends! As Reed's youth pastor, I CONFRONTED HIM and WARNED HIM about how important it was for him to stay connected to other Christians through the youth group. *But Reed just distanced himself further from the youth group and eventually stopped going altogether.*

Reed came over one night and **told me how he had started using drugs**. He said he **COULDN'T STOP**. My heart broke. I knew he did not plan to take this road, but *each little choice he had made to cope with the pain and disappointment he was feeling had led him further down this path.* I had no special formula or message I could pull of of my hip pocket to help him. I was just truly broken for him. I prayed for him. **REED EVENTUALLY GOT KICKED OUT OF SCHOOL.** He's now been in trouble with the law for stealing to support his drug habit. He's lost most of his chances for ever getting a degree. He's emotionally separated from God, family, friends, and church. **He can't hold a job** *and continues to use drugs.*

I can honestly say that Reed never "**INTENDED**" to take this road. **He didn't say "I THINK I WILL TRY DOPE THIS WEEK."** Drugs were never the way Reed **DECIDED** to cope with his problems. **THE MESS HIS LIFE IS IN NOW IS A RESULT OF MANY SMALL CHOICES.**

OPTIONS

SESSION TWO

EXTRA ACTION

STEP 1 - TWIZZLE
"Twizzle" into coping or cop-out positions.

Have students circle up and face clockwise. Introduce this terminology: "Go" means walk in the direction you are facing. "Stop" means freeze! "Turn" means make a half turn (180°) and freeze. "Jump" means jump, make a half-turn, and freeze. "Twizzle" means jump, make a full (360°) turn, and freeze in either the cope position (hold your arms up like a muscle man) or the cop out position (cover your head with your arms). Get students warmed up by calling out the above directions in random order. Then add this wrinkle: Each time you stay stop, read one of the the "coping mechanisms" off Resource 5 and yell "Twizzle." Students decide whether the item read was an example of coping or copping out and get into the appropriate position. Each round, have a few students share why they chose to pose how they did. (Needed: copies of Resource 5.)

STEP 4 - BLIND WALK
Partners guide each other to the stations.

Use Step 4 as written with these variations: Have students partner up. Blindfold one student in each pair. The unblindfolded partner must guide the other from one station to the next. He or she can only touch the partner's one open palm with his or her own palm and must make up a set of signals (for example, pull down for stop, pull left to turn left, and so on). While traveling from station to station partners should discuss what they just learned at the previous station. Rotate which partner is blindfolded at each station. At the end of the activity, add these comments: **Think what would have happened today had your guide not been present and you had to navigate the room blindfolded. That's sometimes the way we try to live life—we go our own way without Christ, our guide! No wonder we end up lost. But Jesus promises to walk with us and guide us if we trust Him.** (Needed: supplies listed in Step 4.)

SMALL GROUP

STEP 3 - BIBLE JEOPARDY
You give students the answers; they give you the questions.

For a fresh approach to God's promises to help us through life, write the Bible references listed in Step 3 on a chalkboard, white board, or somewhere else where students can see them. Next, call out a life situation. Students race to look up the verses and give the promise that corresponds to the life situation. For example, you would say, "Problem: Facing trials or struggles in your life." Students would then search the references listed on the board. The correct answer, er, question, would be, "What is James 1:2-5?" After each round, discuss: **What is promised in this verse? How can you cope with life by living out what this verse says?** (Needed: Bibles, newsprint, marker.)

STEP 4 - PRAY IN ACTION
Mobilize your students to put accountability into action.

Instead of setting up four stations, give each student a blank sheet of paper and have them write the "PRAY" acronym vertically down the left side of their page. Discuss what each letter stands for in detail. Use the activities and discussion questions included in the PRAY stations but go through them as a group. Encourage your students to be honest and discuss their questions, doubts, and personal experiences with each aspect of the PRAY strategy. When you get to the accountability section, instead of just saying accountability is important, consider assigning accountability partners for the upcoming week and challenge your students to hold each other accountable to put the PRAY strategy in action. Conclude by telling students that next week you will ask: 1) Who put PRAY into practice and how? and 2) Who followed through and talked to their accountability partners? (Needed: newsprint, marker.)

LARGE GROUP

STEP 1 - AMERICAN EAGLE
Students try to get across the room without being picked up.

For an activity that will get more students involved, clear a large playing area—preferably in a gym or outside. Have all students line up at one end of the court. Have your adult leaders stand around center court. Say: **When I say go, your goal is to get to the other side of the court (field, etc.) without being picked up off the ground by one of your leaders. You are "out" if you are picked up and both feet leave the ground and the person (or people) picking you up yell, "American Eagle!" When that happens, you become one of the people trying to pick up the runners for the rest of the game until everyone has been grabbed.** Have students run back and forth until all have been picked up. For obvious reasons you might want to run two separate games—one for girls and one for guys. (Needed: large playing area.)

STEP 3 - SMALL STUDIES
Students study the Bible passages in small groups.

You can adapt the Bible study in Step 3 for a large group in several ways. First, divide your students into groups of no more than four and assign them all of the passages in Step 3. Or, you could have each small group discuss the verse's significance with their own small group. (Needed: Bibles.)

41

OPTIONS

SESSION TWO

HEARD IT ALL BEFORE

STEP 3 - WHY DOESN'T IT WORK?
Challenge students to ask tough questions and go beyond "right" answers.

This option will require you to take some risks and it may raise more questions than it answers. (Jesus often did that.) Use Step 3 as directed but add an important element of discussion: The three passages listed in Step 3 will be familiar to church kids. Ask students to recall times when they didn't find the connection between the problem and the promise to be quite that simple. Start with the Philippians passage—it may be the least threatening, then move to the James passage, and finally to Hebrews. Discuss the factors that may have contributed to the promises not working. For example, maybe students misinterpreted the promise, or they were not willing to wait for God's answer, or perhaps they didn't take the issue very seriously. Help students see what a real, honest walk with God is—not always having all the answers but trusting and growing closer to God all the time.

STEP 4 - TV ADS FOR PRAY
Make TV ads to promote each of the four steps in the PRAY strategy.

Put your students in four small groups as the original idea suggests, but instead of having them rotate through the stations, assign each group just one of the four steps. Groups should prepare and produce a 30-second TV commercial that promotes the specific step they've been assigned. Either have the students perform their commercials "live" or videotape them and watch them on a TV/VCR unit. *(Needed: TV, VCR, blank videotape, video camera.)*

LITTLE BIBLE BACKGROUND

STEP 1 - WAS IT EASIER THEN?
Don't let students get away with thinking life was easier in Bible times.

Use Step 1 as directed, then debate these questions: **Is it harder to cope with life today than in Jesus' time? What were the pressures faced by young people in Israel all those years ago? How did they cope? Were they faced with the temptation to drink or do drugs? Did they live in an easier time or were they somehow stronger than people today?** The fact is, life was every bit as difficult then as now. Don't allow anyone in your group to cop out by claiming it's harder to cope now. The Bible's prescription for coping, which is what this session is about, is totally sufficient to deal with modern trials.

STEP 4 - GOD IS OUR POWER
Make sure students don't miss the fact that God is the power in the PRAY strategy.

Impress upon your group that the PRAY strategy includes the steps students need to take to reach the source of the power to succeed: God. In other words, it is God who brings victory over drugs and other issues, not us. Each of the steps in the PRAY strategy is designed to help a student achieve a healthy, vibrant relationship with the One who can destroy the power of temptation and addiction. Without this relationship, the motivation to live a godly life and the ability to do so are not there. This is a good time to present the way of salvation if there are students in your group who may never have given themselves fully to Him.

FELLOWSHIP & WORSHIP

STEP 2 - HOW DO YOU COPE?
Students build deeper relationships by sharing answers to tough coping questions.

Instead of using the "Coping Quotes" activity, divide students into small groups of four to six students. Tell them to discuss more personal, in-depth questions that will help breed deeper fellowship, like: **What's one problem you're going through right now that's tough to deal with? What do you "feel" like doing in response to the problem? How are you really coping with the problem? What can this group do to help you learn and grow from your struggles?**

STEP 4 - A PRAYER AND A PROMISE
Students meditate on a powerful prayer.

After working through the PRAY stations, gather students in a circle on the floor. Turn the lights down low. Read the following prayer and encourage students to personalize, reflect on, and meditate on the words: **Lord, there are times when I try so hard, but still fail, and times when I feel so discouraged I want to quit. There are times when I feel betrayed by my friends and hurt by my parents. There are times when I haven't remained pure and the guilt weighs heavy on me. There are times when I feel like giving in, giving up, and checking out. But then I remember the scars on Your brow, the stripes on Your back, the nails in Your hands, and the spear in Your side. And I remember . . . You've been there. And You're here to help me in my time of need. Thank you, Lord, for loving even me.** While students remain in a reflective mood, read Hebrews 4:15-16. Close by singing several songs that deal with trusting God such as: "You Are My Hiding Place" or "Thy Word." *(Needed: Bible.)*

OPTIONS

SESSION TWO

MOSTLY GIRLS

STEP 1 - GIRLS' COPING ISSUES
Add more girl issues to the game.

Here are two additional ways girls sometimes cope with life. Put these two on index cards and add them to the list of coping mechanisms on Resource 5 for use in the "Coping" game:
- Clue word: Under-eating. Off-limit List: diet, skipping meals, starving, purging.
- Clue word: Escaping. Off-limit List: shopping, TV, talking on the phone, video games. *(Needed: index cards, pen, cut-out copies of Resource 5.)*

STEP 4 - GIRLS' NIGHT OUT
Plan a special evening, possibly a retreat, to continue talking about coping.

This session would be great to use as a springboard for further discussion in the context of an overnighter or day away. Use Step 4 as directed, then invite the girls to help you plan a "Girls Night Out," an overnighter held either at the church or a retreat center. In the last few minutes of the meeting, girls can offer their suggestions and input but many of the following suggestions will require your leadership and direction outside of the meeting time. Ideas: Design different activities geared toward helping the girls have a healthy self-image both internally and externally. Possible ideas are: have a "mini-spa" where a physical trainer talks about the benefit of keeping in shape, for example, how being physically fit reduces a person's stress level and how girls have a healthier worldview when they are physically active; bring in a makeup artist to teach how to do facials/manicures and see if they can bring in samples. Also, bring in a local counselor (preferably female and Christian) who specializes in working with teenage girls and have her talk about how to develop healthy coping strategies.

MOSTLY GUYS

STEP 1 - GUYS' COPING ISSUES
Add more guy issues to the Taboo game.

Although guys definitely use the coping mechanisms listed in Resource 5, there are a couple of other mechanisms you might want to add to the list that are specific to guys. Put these on index cards and add them to the list from Resource 5 for use in the "Coping" game:
- Clue Word: Burying It. Off-limit List: bury, forget, dead, tomb, casket. (This issue refers to the idea that guys don't want others to know they are struggling, so they bury the issue by acting like nothings wrong.)
- Clue Word: Too Cool. Off-limit List: cool, cucumber, happening, above it. (This issue refers to the idea that guys will put on airs as if they are above the fray of life's problems. Guys don't like to look weak, especially not around other guys.) *(Needed: index cards, pen, cut-out copies of Resource 5.)*

STEP 3 - THE LUST PROBLEM
Discuss the problem of lust and a promise from God to help guys.

One of the most prevalent problems teenage guys face is lust. Use Step 3 as directed, but add this discussion as well: Have your guys look up Matthew 5:27-28. Include this in your discussion of problems—the problem here, of course, is lust. Then talk about God's promise. Read 1 Corinthians 10:13. Ask guys to put this verse in their own words. *(Needed: supplies listed in Step 3.)*

EXTRA FUN

STEP 1 - YOU COULD . . .
Students randomly match problem cards with a list of foolish responses.

Ask your students to come up with some really DUMB things that people do that get them in trouble or mess up their lives. Pass out index cards and ask students to write down a dumb thing on each card. Each example should start out with "You could . . ." (Example: You could take a swing at a cop.) Collect all the cards and put them in a container. Then, have your students brainstorm a list of problems that people face from time to time, write each on a slip of paper, and deposit in a container. For example: a broken heart, failure to make the team, rejection by friends, feeling left out or insignificant, and so on. Now, match the problem from one container with the dumb example from the other. Could be very funny and sometimes very accurate! Discuss: **What are some healthy ways to deal with your problems—instead of just picking a foolish idea out of a hat?**

STEP 4 - ENCOURAGEMENT CHEERS
Suggestions for ways students can cheer one another on.

When others encourage us, we often can handle situations that would otherwise really mess up our minds. Here are a number of ways you could provide opportunities for students to encourage one another:
- Have students create and give cheers for one another (example: Ra, Ra, Roo, Roo, there's no one like Mary Lou. A great big smile and warm hello makes you want to stay and never go!)
- Have students write encouraging letters to one another. Ask them to incorporate the biblical promises studied in Step 3. *(Needed: variable.)*

OPTIONS

SESSION TWO

MEDIA

STEP 2 - COSTLY COPING
Create coping vignettes.

It's OK to have a lot of fun while making a serious point! First, brainstorm with your "actors" some typical ways teenagers cope with their struggles today. List five or six good ones. Next, figure out how you and your group can depict these in one or two minute vignettes. Practice for a few minutes. Get your camera cued and then have the students act out the vignettes one at a time. When you're done, set up the TV so that these can be shown to the whole group. Stop after each individual vignette and discuss each one. *(Needed: TV, VCR, video camera, videotape.)*

STEP 4 - CREATIVE COPING
Create coping vignettes.

Again, brainstorm with your students some healthy, appropriate ways to cope with difficult drug-related situations. After coming up with five or six, determine how these can be acted out on camera. Then, act it out and videotape it for your group. That night, show to your group these more appropriate forms of handling these situations. You can stop after each one and discuss it. To end this segment, read Hebrews 4:15 together. *(Needed: TV, VCR, video camera, videotape.)*

SHORT MEETING TIME

STEP 1 - SPEED PICTIONARY
Draw coping mechanisms and ask students to guess them.

Instead of waiting for all the students to arrive to play "Don't Get Buzzed," begin by drawing on a chalkboard or piece of newsprint pictures and symbols to represent as many coping mechanisms as you can think of. Begin by drawing those listed on Resource 5. Let students compete to be the first to guess what you're drawing. Use the discussion questions at the end of Step 1.

STEP 2 - SKIP THE DISCUSSION
Skip to a reading of Resource 7.

The "Coping Quotes" activity is a good idea but it may take up too much time. Instead, start Step 2 by reading as dramatically as you can the story of Reed ("Choices," Resource 7, page 39). Use the discussion questions at the end of Step 2.

STEP 4 - PRAY FROM UPFRONT
Skip the stations. Discuss the PRAY strategy as a class.

Instead of spending the time to divide into groups and walk around to different stations, present the information, activities, and discussion questions for each station.

URBAN

STEP 1 - TIGHT SQUEEZE
Put the squeeze on one student to make a point.

The city has many pressures which can lead teens to use drugs abuse. Illustrate this by asking for a volunteer who can take the pressure of a big group squeeze. Have all students squeeze-in on the volunteer for five seconds. Be sure teens know that when the five seconds are up they must immediately break up the squeeze. Next, ask for three students who want to protect the volunteer during the next squeeze. Have the three volunteers circle themselves as a barrier around the student to be squeezed. The role of the three volunteers is to keep the group pressure off of the student in the middle. Again, have everyone "Squeeze!" for five seconds and head back to their seats. Discuss: **Was the first or second squeeze tighter? Why?** Finally, relate the activity to the fact that all Christians have an assurance of full pressure-protection from God. God doesn't remove the negative aspects of life's pressure, but He keeps it from overtaking us.

STEP 4 - URBAN JUSTIFICATION
Help students list justifications as to why they should or shouldn't be Christians.

City teens constantly need to justify why Christianity is right because of the public skepticism true believers face. Another way to do this activity is to simply have students justify the importance of each station and to give five hip-pocket justifications as to why a believer should be dedicated to each.

OPTIONS

SESSION TWO

COMBINED

STEP 2 - COP-OUT CULTURE
Teams race to find four words to describe how Jesus treated His friends.

After using the "Coping Quotes" activity as directed, make a list of all the people who they know who have "copped out" of their problems by using drugs and alcohol. For example, students could list friends, family members, musicians (Elvis Presley, members of the Rolling Stones, Kurt Kobain), celebrities (John Belushi, Kelsey Grammer, Robert Downey Jr., Robin Williams), and professional athletes (Steve Howe, Michael Ervin, Leon Lett, Tony Phillips). In as many situations as you have time for, discuss how using drugs and alcohol simply made the abusers' problems worse, not better. This activity can replace the reading of the "Choices" story (Resource 7).

STEP 4 - ACTION APPLICATION
Groups of students act out an application of one of the stations.

To help make this step more engaging for a combined group of junior and senior highers, end the fourth rotation right after students move to that fourth station. Explain that you've chosen to end it early because you've got an even better idea. You want each group of students to make up either a funny or serious drama about the station that they're in right now to help the rest of the students understand the role that station plays in healthy coping. Every student gets to be involved. Give each group 8-10 minutes to design their drama and then ask each group to perform their drama sketch before the rest of the group. *(Needed: supplies listed in Step 4.)*

EXTRA CHALLENGE

STEP 3 - CONQUERORS
Study how Paul overcame many tough problems.

Begin the Bible study by asking: **What is the difference between a pinball and a car? How is "trying to cope" like living like a pinball? If we were to truly live for God, how could that be like driving a car?** Supplement students' answers by saying: **If Christ is firmly on the throne of our lives, we won't have to just "cope" in the same way others do; we can see circumstances as tools in God's hand to shape us in His image. We can be like the car—driven and propelled to reach our goal, and not like the pinball—bounced around by gears and levers.** Read 2 Corinthians 11:16—12:20 together. Discuss: **How would Paul react to the drug use in today's culture? How was Paul a "conqueror," much more than merely a "cope-er"? What behavior or attitude will have to change in your life to make you a conqueror? What problem would you like to conquer in your life?** Leave students a few minutes of silence to ponder the last two questions on their own.

STEP 4 - EXTENDED PRAYER
Pray for each other to be conquerors.

Go through the PRAY stations as directed, but refer back to the Bible study above and instead of calling PRAY a coping strategy, call it a conquering strategy. After the PRAY stations, gather together and close together by praying for one another. Challenge students to be honest about their answers to the question: *What needs to change in your life for you to become a conqueror?* When a student shares, encourage the rest of the group to respond by praying for him or her right there on the spot.

PLANNING CHECKLIST

STEP 1 (5-10 MIN. UNLESS NOTED)
- ❑ **Extra Action:** Twizzle
- ❑ **Large Group:** American Eagle
- ❑ **Little Bible:** Was It Easier Then?
- ❑ **Mostly Girls:** Girls' Coping Issues
- ❑ **Mostly Guys:** Guys' Coping Issues
- ❑ **Extra Fun:** You Could . . .
- ❑ **Short Time:** Speed Pictionary (3-5 min.)
- ❑ **Urban:** Tight Squeeze

STEP 2 (10-15 MIN. UNLESS NOTED)
- ❑ **Fellowship & Worship:** How Do You Cope?
- ❑ **Media:** Costly Coping
- ❑ **Short Time:** Skip the Discussion (5-10 min.)
- ❑ **Combined:** Cop Out Culture

STEP 3 (15-20 MIN. UNLESS NOTED)
- ❑ **Small Group:** Bible Jeopardy
- ❑ **Large Group:** Small Studies
- ❑ **Heard It All:** Why Doesn't It Work?
- ❑ **Mostly Guys:** The Lust Problem
- ❑ **Extra Challenge:** Conquerors

STEP 4 (10-15 MIN. UNLESS NOTED)
- ❑ **Extra Action:** Blind Walk
- ❑ **Small Group:** PRAY in Action
- ❑ **Heard It All:** TV Ads for PRAY
- ❑ **Little Bible:** God Is Our Power
- ❑ **Fellowship & Worship:** A Prayer and A Promise
- ❑ **Mostly Girls:** Girls' Night Out
- ❑ **Extra Fun:** Encouragement Cheers
- ❑ **Media:** Creative Coping
- ❑ **Short Time:** PRAY from Upfront (5-10 min.)
- ❑ **Urban:** Urban Justification
- ❑ **Combined:** Action Application
- ❑ **Extra Challenge:** Extended Prayer

SESSION 3

But It's Not That Easy to Just Say No

YOUR GOALS FOR THIS SESSION:
Choose one or more

☐ To help students realize that there is no quick fix to stay drug free in today's world.

☐ To help students understand that God can give them the power to stay off drugs and alcohol.

☐ To challenge students to develop real-life strategies and action plans to help them stay off drugs and alcohol.

☐ Other: _____

Your Bible Base:

1 Corinthians 10:13
Romans 7:19-20; 8:1-4
Hebrews 4:15-16; 12:1-3

CUSTOM CURRICULUM

STEP 1

Quick Fixes

In "Quick Fixes," students create gadgets to fix tough problems: 5-10 minutes. Or, choose one of the option categories highlighted in the left sidebar and see pages 57-61 for more "Getting Together" options.

Supplies needed: random items, paper bag, copies of Resource 8, "Problem Cards" (page 53).
Set up: Cut out copies of Resource 8 and put the "Problem Cards" into a paper bag. Choose four volunteers.

Each volunteer should pick a "gadget" (one of the random items you brought in—anything from a stirring spoon to a football) and a Problem Card. Instruct volunteers to create a 30-second commercial proclaiming how their gadget can fix the particular problem on their card. Judge the best presentation with an "applause meter." Give one of your gadgets away as a prize.

Can you think of any examples in real life where people try to apply "quick fixes" to tough problems? (instant weight-loss pills, get-rich-quick schemes, instant muscle drinks, *Cliff Notes*.)

Let's take the problem of staying off drugs and alcohol. Is that an easy problem or a hard one?

What kinds of "quick fixes" do you hear to the problem of drugs and alcohol? Do these quick fixes usually work? Why or why not?

Wouldn't it be great if all we had to do to stay "drug free" was get the right "gadget"? Unfortunately, real life doesn't work like that, does it? For example, there's no magic wand that will help you stay off drugs, is there? Staying drug free in the real world is much more difficult.

OPTIONS

- EXTRA ACTION
- SMALL GROUP
- LARGE GROUP
- MOSTLY GUYS
- MEDIA
- SHORT MEETING TIME

S E S S I O N T H R E E

STEP 2

Get Real?

Below, two students act out a mini-drama about turning down drugs and the group discusses what a realistic scenario would be: 10-15 minutes. Or, choose one of the option categories highlighted in the right sidebar and see pages 57-61 for more "Getting Thirsty" options.

Supplies needed: two copies of Resource 9, "Everybody's Doing It" (page 54), for actors.
Set up: Prepare two actors ahead of time with copies of Resource 9. Encourage them to memorize and rehearse the mini-drama.

You can introduce the drama by saying something like: **What's your experience been in terms of saying no to drugs and alcohol? Here's one scenario for you to consider.** Cue your actors to perform the drama, then discuss:

Was this a realistic conversation? Why or why not?

Do you like what Dave had to say when he was offered drugs? Why or why not?

Would you have said anything different than Dave in handling the situation? If so, what?

What would be the hardest thing about being in Dave's situation or any other situation in which you are offered drugs or alcohol?

Conclude by saying something like: **On any given weekend, it can seem like "everybody's doin' it"—like all your peers are drinking, partying, or using drugs of some kind. Is it realistic for you to go through high school without getting caught up in the party scene at some point? It may be difficult. But it's not impossible. Let's see what the Bible has to say.**

OPTIONS

- FELLOWSHIP & WORSHIP
- MOSTLY GIRLS
- URBAN
- JR. HIGH / HIGH SCHOOL COMBINED

CUSTOM CURRICULUM

STEP 3

Three Groups and a Bible

Below, students get into three groups where they hear a promise from Scripture that God will give them the power to stay drug free: 15-20 minutes. Or, choose one of the option categories highlighted in the left sidebar and see pages 57-61 for more "Getting the Word" options.

Supplies needed: index cards, pens, Bibles, cut-out copies of Resource 10, "Roleplay Cards" (page 55).

Set up: Recruit three adult volunteers or mature students to lead each group. Use the directions below to prepare your leaders in advance to lead a short activity and a brief follow-up roleplay in their groups. Set up three areas in your room for each group. Divide your students into three small groups.

Each group should spend five minutes interacting with their Bible passage and then use the rest of the time preparing their roleplay for the group.

Group 1—*What students read:* I Corinthians 10:13. *What students do:* Write down on index cards times when they believe God provided for them a "way out" of a tempting situation dealing with drugs and alcohol. *What students roleplay:* Give each student a copy of the roleplay card from Resource 10 that deals with their group's Bible passage. Give them five minutes to create and present a roleplay based on the card.

Group 2—*What students read:* Romans 7:19-20; 8:1-4. *What students do:* Write a short letter to God on index cards describing any struggle they're having or have had with drugs and alcohol, and asking Him for the power to win that struggle. (If drugs and alcohol is not a problem, students may write a letter to God discussing some other issue they struggle with for which it is difficult to say no.) *What students roleplay:* Give each student a copy of the roleplay card from Resource 10 that deals with their group's Bible passage. Give them five minutes to create and present a roleplay based on the card.

Group 3—*What students read:* Hebrews 4:15-16. *What students do:* Write a paraphrase of the verse; in other words, put the verse in their own words. In this station it is particularly important that the leader be ready to offer his or her explanation of the verse. Equip the station leader to close this station by emphasizing the fact that Jesus understands the temptations we go through; He had complete victory over temptation, and that means all of us can go to Him to receive help when we are struggling with drugs and alcohol. *What students roleplay:* Give each student a copy of the roleplay card from Resource 10 that deals with their group's Bible passage. Give them five minutes to create and present a roleplay based on the card.

Keep the groups where they are, but have them send up their drama teams to present their Bible passage and roleplay.

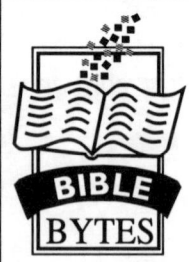

The Role of the Holy Spirit's Power
Various Scripture

- ◆ **SCRIPTURE BYTES:** Some disciplined people may be able to stay drug free without the power of the Holy Spirit, but no one can please God on his or her own (Romans 9:17). Paul says that we shouldn't have any "confidence in the flesh"; our nature is to do what is pleasurable, even if it's sinful (1 Corinthians 5:17; Romans 8:7). Sometimes the Holy Spirit will work by giving leadings, which have been described by many people as "impressions on the heart" (1 Samuel 8:19; Acts 12:54-56). Other times the Holy Spirit will convict, which means He will give us a strong sense that what we're about to do is wrong.
- ◆ **BYTE-SIZE INSIGHTS:** If you want to teach your students to be drug free, the best thing you can teach them is how to depend on the Holy Spirit. Remind students that there is nothing they can't handle with God's help.

STEP 4

www.drug.free

Below, groups of students design and present a home page for a web site that will help other students choose to be drug free: 10-15 minutes. Or, choose one of the option categories highlighted in the left sidebar and see pages 57-61 for more "Getting the Point" options.

OPTIONS

- SMALL GROUP
- HEARD IT ALL BEFORE
- EXTRA FUN
- MEDIA
- URBAN

Supplies needed: overhead projector, overhead pens, transparencies.
Set up: Keep your students in the same three groups from Step 3.

Have your three groups of students create a concept for a web site that can be used to help their peers be drug free. As they develop their concepts, hand each group overhead pens of different colors and an overhead transparency.

Explain: **Your job now is to take what you have learned from your Bible passage and your roleplay and design the home page for a web site. Your web site's address is up to you. Just make it practical and attractive. You will present the page to the rest of the group in seven minutes. Have fun!**

After each group has shown their home page on the overhead projector, discuss: **Why should your friends care about God's help to stay drug free? How can you talk to them about it?**

SESSION THREE

STEP 5

Prayer Cards

Below, students fill out anonymous prayer cards and commit to pray for another student: 5-10 minutes.
Or, choose one of the option categories highlighted in the right sidebar and see pages 57-61 for more "Getting Personal" options.

Supplies needed: index cards, pencils.
Set up: Pass out index cards and pencils.

Asking for prayer from their peers is a huge step for most teens. But if you can begin to teach your students to pray for one another, there's no better way to build community in your group.

Tell students to take a few minutes to write down a prayer request about a situation dealing with drugs and alcohol. For example, students might write: *I need help to know what to say when someone offers me drugs* or *I need help to know what to do when students call me a loser for not doing drugs.* You can encourage students to put their names on the cards, but do not require it. Collect the cards, then distribute them randomly. Challenge students to make a two-week commitment to pray once a day for the person whose card they received. Close your time by leaving a few minutes for students to pray silently for the person whose card they have.

OPTIONS
- EXTRA ACTION
- LITTLE BIBLE BACKGROUND
- FELLOWSHIP & WORSHIP
- MOSTLY GIRLS
- EXTRA FUN
- EXTRA CHALLENGE

THE DRUG FREE CHALLENGE

QUICK FIX CARDS

Problem #1
ALWAYS LOSING THINGS
You keep losing things like your car keys, wallet/purse, homework, little brother, Bible, jacket, etc.

Problem #2
EMBARRASSING NOISES
You have a habit of making uncontrollable and obnoxious noises at the most embarrassing times.

Problem #3
BROKEN STEREO
Your stereo broke and you need something to fix it.

Problem #4
HEADACHES
It never fails. Every time you sit down in English class, you get a splitting headache.

Problem #5
CAN'T REMEMBER NAMES
You keep forgetting names of people you know.

Problem #6
BREAKING UP
You need help breaking up with your girlfriend/boyfriend.

THE DRUG FREE CHALLENGE

Everybody's Doing It!

RESOURCE 9

STEVE: Are you coming to the party tonight?

DAVE: Yeah, I'll be there.

STEVE: It seemed like you had a good time last week. Were you drunk or what?

DAVE: No. I just had a couple of beers. I don't think I'll even drink tonight.

STEVE: How come? Everybody's doing it.

DAVE: I'm a Christian. I made a mistake last week. I'm suppose to have higher standards.

STEVE: (still not quite getting it) Well, how about pot? I've got a sample for you, if you want. You'll have a great time with this tonight!

DAVE: Thanks Steve, but I don't think so. I like to hang out with everyone, but I just don't want to get messed up with drugs or alcohol.

Steve: You won't get messed up. Heck, I've been doin' drugs and getting drunk all through high school . . . and look at me! (smiling, like he's doing great)

Dave: (sarcastically positive) Yeah, look at you. Well, I have to go. See ya' next week.

Steve: What about the party tonight?

Dave: Like I said, see ya' next week.

Steve: Okay, but it's your loss.

Dave: I don't think so, Steve. I just don't think so.

THE DRUG FREE CHALLENGE

RESOURCE 10

Roleplay Cards

1 Corinthians 10:13
We have God's power to run from temptation: God will always provide a way of escape. Roleplay a situation where someone is offering you drugs or alcohol. The pressure to give in is high, but you simply say "No!" and walk away.

Romans 7:19-20, 8:1-4
We have God's power to help us when we struggle: Despite your resolve to stay drug free, it's impossible without God's help. Roleplay a situation where a friend invites you to "hang out" at a party where there will be drugs. You respond by choosing to do something fun, somewhere else.

Hebrews 4:15-16
We can ask for help, and God's power, when we seek it: Trying to handle a serious struggle drug or alcohol on your own just won't work. Roleplay a situation where a person struggling with drug use finally goes to a respected peer or adult and seeks his or her advice and help.

THE DRUG FREE CHALLENGE
Internet Threads

optional RESOURCE 11

Jessi345: Mad...hey, what's up?
MadDogJD: Not too much here, you?
Jessi345: I dunno...I was invited to this party.
MadDogJD: That's kewl, so what's the problem?
Psalm23: What kind of party is this Jessi????
Jessi345: Well...a lot of my friends are gonna be there, so I wanna go...but I know there's gonna be drinkin too, and I'm not into that.
MadDogJD: DRINKIN! Right On!
Cutie6234: That's a tough issue. My personal belief is it's not wrong to drink unless you get drunk.
Psalm23: Yeah, but it's against the law if you're under age. How old are you?
Jessi345: I'm 17. Well, I'm not sure if I wanna go and hang out...or what?

Nuhtcase: Anyways, so this guy at school stuck a joint in my face the other day and I hardly even knew him.
Arrielle: Really? That goes on at my school all the time, too.
Wildman4U: I'm not into any of that. I've told a lot of people no at my school. Now I got a reputation as a goodie goodie.
Arielle: Doesn't that make you feel like a loser????
Wildman4U: Yeah, sometimes.
Nuhtcase: I hate that. It's like...you do it or your a loser. I wish there was something else I could say.

Angel1285: I'm tired of the drinking and smoking at my school. It's like people don't have anything better to do.
BearClawz: If they want to drink or smoke...you should respect their decision.
Angel1285: I think they're all losers.
MarkoPolo: I'm not a loser...I'm a good Christian...most of the time. But when I get around my friends who party, God seems to slip my mind.
Angel1285: You make it sound like they make you drink or something??? If you were really a good Christian, you wouldn't let God slip your mind. I don't.

OPTIONS

SESSION THREE

EXTRA ACTION

STEP 1 - NO QUICK FIXES
Design and produce commercials for "quick fix" products.

Choose one student to be the communicator and give him or her a piece of paper with a design on it. Without showing the group the design, the communicator must effectively describe the design so that the rest of the class can duplicate it on their own papers. This activity would make a good lead-in to the discussion at the end of Step 1. *(Needed: paper, pens.)*

STEP 5 - PRAYER STONES
Students tie their prayer requests to stones.

Give each student a medium-size stone, a pen, a piece of paper, and a rubber band. Tell students to write out an ending to this sentence: "When it comes to drugs, alcohol, or the whole party scene, I need prayer for _____." Have students fold up the note, wrap it around the stone with the rubber band, and throw the stone and note into a pile in the center of the room. Say: **The house that you live in is built upon a rock solid foundation. The foundation is made up of thousands of tiny stones that make it strong. It is the same way with prayer! Our foundation is made up of thousands of tiny stones that make it strong. It is the same way with prayer! Our everyday prayers are like tiny stones that make up the foundation of our lives. Also . . . when we pray for someone else we are helping them build a strong and solid foundation.** Have your students grab a stone from the center of the pile, making sure that they don't grab their own. Challenge them to place the stone in their room at home where they can see it. The stone will be a reminder that they are to pray once a day for the person whose note was attached. *(Needed: stones, paper, pens, and rubberbands.)*

SMALL GROUP

STEP 1 - QUICK FIX STORM
Teams brainstorm lists of quick fixes.

As you probably know, putting students on the spot in a small group is a dangerous proposition. Students can feel extremely awkward and the activity can quickly backfire on you. Instead, have students pair up and charge them to come up with as many examples of "quick fixes" as they can in three minutes. After three minutes, have pairs read their lists. Give pairs one point for each item listed that did not appear on anyone else's list. To transition to the rest of the lesson, tell the group you will throw out a saying and they should throw back at you what problem the slogan is meant to be a "quick fix" for "Just Say No." Students will of course know this refers to turning down drugs. Use the discussion questions at the end of Step 1. *(Needed: paper, pens.)*

STEP 4 - SEARCH ENGINE
In small teams, create a listing of possible drug-free web sites.

Instead of having several groups create several web sites, have your group of students create an Internet search engine. A search engine is similar to a telephone book, except it groups web sites by function and/or topic giving you a quick and easy way to access whatever sites you're searching for. Have your students create directories and topic listings for their directory of drug-free sites. Then, have them create the name, look, and web address of their search engine. You'll find that your students already have the ability to access and organize several pieces of information to help them and their friends be drug free. *(Needed: paper, pens.)*

LARGE GROUP

STEP 1 - PROBLEM PICTIONARY
Play the drawing/guessing game "Pictionary" and use a "quick fix" theme.

Ahead of time, prepare an overhead transparency, screen transparencies, and marking pens for each team. Write 10 things that have to do with "fixing," each on one index card (for example, wrench, screwdriver, duct tape, calculator, glue, plumber, math teacher, and so on.) Divide into two teams. To begin, each team sends one contestant up front. Show contestants one of the cards, then have them try to draw a picture of that object on the transparency. The first team to guess the word wins that round. Post judges close to each team so they can determine which team guesses the drawing first. Then rotate drawers. Use the transition comments at the end of Step 1. *(Needed: two overhead projectors and screens, box of transparency markers, index cards.)*

STEP 3 - TAG-TEAM TEACHING
Ideas for teaching students the content of the power stations without having to move around the room.

Have students remain seated and pass out pens and paper. A single teacher can teach the group about the four Scripture passages (see Step 3). Or you might wish to have three different teachers handle the teaching in a "tag-team" approach. *(Needed: paper, pens.)*

OPTIONS

SESSION THREE

HEARD IT ALL BEFORE

STEP 3 - THEY WRITE THE STUDY
Students prepare a Bible study for a fictional audience.

Your students are probably ready to put some of their wisdom and experience into practice. Move them into three groups (or multiples of three if your group is large), and ask them to imagine that they are leading a voluntary attendance Bible Study in a Juvenile Detox Center with a group of adolescents who genuinely want to kick their drug or alcohol habit. Have each group prepare four or five discussion starting questions on their passage of Scripture. Encourage them to add any other related passages that might be helpful. *(Needed: paper, pens, Bibles.)*

STEP 4 - INTERNET THREADS
Respond to "threads" from the Internet with advice about drugs and alcohol.

Take a fresh approach to get students' attention. Pass out copies of the optional Resource 11, "Internet Threads" (page 56). Most of your students will be familiar with what "chat rooms" are on the Internet. But you may need to explain the concept to others. Chat rooms are a way of having electronic conversations with people from across the world who, via their computer and phone line, arrive at the same electronic address. During the course of the conversation, what one person types and sends on his or her computer shows up on another person's computer screen. Resource 11 contains three of these electronic conversations. The addresses, or names, have been changed. Discuss with students: **If you were on the Internet right now, what would you write back? Why?** If time permits, let students write out their advice on Resource 11 and let volunteers share what they wrote. *(Needed: copies of Resource 11, pens.)*

LITTLE BIBLE BACKGROUND

STEP 3 - JESUS' TEMPTATION
Discuss what difference it makes knowing Jesus faced temptation like we did.

Hebrews 4:15 tells us that our Savior was tempted in every way, just as we are. Students may question whether or not Jesus faced the exact same pressures to use drugs that they face. Did Jesus' schoolmates try to con Him into using the latest designer drugs? There is no such record in Scripture, but there is a text that reveals how Jesus dealt with a different temptation. Matthew 4:1-11 gives a detailed account of Christ's temptation. There are many lessons to be learned here, including the importance of following faithfully wherever God's Spirit leads, the reality of Satan's involvement in temptation (including substance abuse), and the need to use the Bible as a weapon against temptation. Take a moment to read the passage aloud and discuss these points with your class. *(Needed: Bibles.)*

STEP 5 - FORGIVENESS DISCUSSION
Discuss God's grace.

Some of the anonymous prayer cards may reveal that one or more students have done drugs and are in trouble. Point out that sins—even substance abuse and addiction—can be forgiven by God. He stands ready to do so as we confess (see 1 John 1:9). At the conclusion of the activity, allow your class a minute of silent prayer during which they can take their sins to God. Close the prayer by thanking God for providing forgiveness to all who ask. Tell your class that you are available to meet with anyone who needs help or advice. Encourage your students to call you if they don't feel comfortable approaching you now. You must be ready to offer help and support to anyone who seeks it. If you do not feel qualified to deal with an addicted student, be sure you know the names of people and organizations who are.

FELLOWSHIP & WORSHIP

STEP 2 - ONE ON ONE
Students find a person they don't know well and discuss a list of questions.

This idea may challenge your students out of their comfort zones a little but the end result is always more positive fellowship. Instruct students to get up and find one person they don't know very well. Encourage them to walk around the room with that person—movement can help eliminate some awkwardness. Throw out general questions about drugs and alcohol that students can review while they walk. For example: **On a scale of 1 (easy) to 10 (very hard) how hard is it for you to say no to alcohol or drugs if they're offered to you? Do you believe relying on God alone can be enough to resist the temptation to experiment with drugs and alcohol? Why do you think so many teens are so tempted to experiment with drugs, smoking, and alcohol?**

STEP 5 - ENCOURAGED BY PRAYER
A team of adults pray for the students.

This step works best if you work with a team of adult volunteers. If that's not the case for you, you might ask a few adults in your church to come to the meeting specifically to make themselves available to pray for students. To close the meeting, ask students to pause wherever they are and reflect upon what the Lord may be speaking to them about in regard to drugs and alcohol. If you can, have a song leader lead the group in several worship choruses and instruct students to sing or pray quietly. Then, make a general invitation to your students to get up and ask one of the adults to pray for them. Dismiss after all have had a chance to be prayed for.

O P T I O N S

S E S S I O N T H R E E

MOSTLY GIRLS

STEP 2 - OPRAH SIN-FREE
Stage a talk show to discuss drugs and alcohol-related issues.

Choose one student to be "Oprah," others to be guests on the show, and the rest to be audience members. Have Guest #1 play the role of a hard-core partyer who has no intention of giving up her lifestyle. Have Guest #2 be a "goodie-goodie" who stays at home crocheting tea cozies (whatever those are). Guest #3 is a recovering partyer who became a Christian and is honest about how hard it was to give up that life. Guest #4 is a Christian who is really attracted to the party lifestyle and is seriously thinking about going to a party this weekend and getting drunk. Let the audience ask questions and interact with the guests. "Oprah" needs to know how to facilitate this kind of discussion and how to draw it to a positive conclusion. At the end, have the girls debrief their reactions/experience. **Did anything happen that made you think differently about the topic of drugs and alcohol? Guests, how did you feel playing roles that did not fit you?**

STEP 5 - QUESTIONS IN A HAT
Put questions in a hat and distribute so each girl can research questions in the coming week.

Pass out index cards and pens. Have girls write down any questions they have about drugs anonymously and put these in a hat. Then pass around the hat and instruct students to draw a card that is not their own. Students should research the problem/question in the upcoming week and come back with an answer. Example: "I have a friend who confides in me that he thinks chewing tobacco won't hurt him because he's not smoking. What do I tell him?" *(Needed: index cards, pencils, hat.)*

MOSTLY GUYS

STEP 1 - MIRACLE PRODUCTS
Design and produce commercials for "quick fix" products.

Divide into three teams. Have one team design and present a 30-second commercial for a powdered protein drink guaranteed to turn weaklings into muscle men overnight! Have a second team design and present a 30-second commercial for a no-fail, get-rich-quick money-making scheme. Have the third team design and present a 30-second commercial for any "miracle" product students can dream up that can solve any number of problems they can think of. Use the discussion questions at the end of Step 1.

STEP 3 - TEMPTATION GROUP
Add a fourth group.

Supplement the activity by adding a fourth group specifically geared to the needs of your guys: *What guys read:* Matthew 4:1-11. *What guys do:* Write a short "critique" letter to Jesus on how He handled temptation; write the letter in a style and voice similar to that you would use to encourage and congratulate a close friend. *What guys roleplay:* Have a few guys act out ways they can use Scripture and follow Jesus' example to overcome temptation. *(Needed: supplies listed in Step 3.)*

EXTRA FUN

STEP 4 - YOU COULD . . . LAUGH
A few fun ideas worth a look.

Use this discussion starter to get the students to think of several light-hearted ways to respond to drugs and alcohol.
- You could . . . crack a joke. Brainstorm funny one-liners students can say when they're offered drugs and alcohol. Humor is a good way to lighten up a tense and tempting situation.
- You could . . . do a whole bunch of things a lot more fun than drugs and alcohol. Every student should know what puts him or her into the "fun zone"—what activities they enjoy and get pleasure out of. The more healthy and fun activities students are involved in, the less they need drugs and alcohol for a good time.
- You could . . . laugh at yourself. Students who are self-confident enough to see the big picture and simply laugh when they get labeled "goodie-goodie" and "prude" are in good shape.
- You could . . . laugh at the "druggies." The idea that a substance could offer you more than God could? Now that's funny!

STEP 5 - T-SHIRTS
Make "Drugs Are For Losers" T-Shirts.

Clothes carry messages. Kids often show their allegiance to an idea, sport, music group, or place by the designs on their T-shirts. Pass out paper and pencils and have your students create designs that would give the message that drugs are for losers. Have them come up with a number of ideas and sketch out the images. Let them know they don't have to be great artists—they just need to get the concept across. Post all the suggestions and vote on which the class would be most likely to wear. Turn over the winner to a kid in the class who is an artist and turn the concept into final art and ultimately T-shirts for the group. *(Needed: white T-shirts, T-shirt paints.)*

OPTIONS

SESSION THREE

MEDIA

STEP 1 - FIX-ALL COMMERCIALS
Tape commercials for quick fix gadgets.

Have fun with the "quick fix" gadget idea in Step 1 by putting the same concept on video. Grab five gadgets from your house, give each gadget a funny name, and determine how these gadgets can be used to fix some significant or completely corny problem. Then videotape five students advertising these gadgets. For example: Call normal stereo headphones "Dr. Eric's Ear Cleaning System." Talk about how Dr. Eric has developed a method by which your ears can be deep cleaned in a painless, effective way. (The content does not have to be great because your students will get a kick out of watching their peers come up with these goofy commercials.) The options are endless! Conclude by using the discussion at the end of Step 1. *(Needed: TV, VCR, video camera, blank tape, various gadgets.)*

STEP 4 - DEAR MOM AND DAD
Tape students' moms and dads giving advice on drug and alcohol.

Here's a great way to include mom and dad into your youth ministry. Set up interview with parents of the kids in your youth group. Be sure not to tell the kids what you're up to! Here's what you do: First, before each interview, videotape (to music) a specific question your students have about drugs and alcohol. For example, print up and videotape for 30 seconds the question, "Should Christian teens go to parties where alcohol is being served?" Then, interview two or three parents and their answers to this question. Do this for five or six questions. Stop the tape after each section and discuss it with your students. The following are good questions to use: What should I say when I'm being offered drugs? How did you deal with drug usage when you were in high school? How can I stay focused on God in tempting situations? What can I do about being labeled a "goodie goodie"? *(Needed: TV, VCR, video camera, blank tape.)*

SHORT MEETING TIME

STEP 1 - IS JUST SAY NO ENOUGH?
Examine various "Just Say No" paraphernalia.

Instead of having an activity ready for students when they arrive, gather as much "Just Say No" paraphernalia as you can. Network with your local government and community organizations. You shouldn't have a problem getting groups to give you items once you tell them what it's for. When students examine the materials, discuss: **How is the slogan "Just Say No" helpful to you? Does it encourage you in any way? How? Does it seem like a quick fix or a true solution to a tough problem? What is a quick fix? What's an example of a realistic strategy for handling a tough problem?** *(Needed: various "Just Say No" materials.)*

STEP 3 - POWER PACKET
Give students concrete reminders of the power of God that's available to them.

If you don't have time to go through all the discussion and activity involved in the groups, give students "power packets" instead—give them tangible reminders of the power of God that's available to them. Once you get done studying the verses listed in Step 3, pass out items like:
• A masonry nail to remind students of the cross and that God uses His power to serve us because of His great love for us.
• A mustard seed to remind students that even faith the size of a mustard seed can be powerful in God's hands.
• A carabiner, used in mountain climbing, to remind students that they are connected to God at all times—God carries them when they start to fall; and there is no challenge too great that they can't tackle it and conquer it with God's help. *(Needed: various items that will work as reminders such as a masonry nails, mustard seeds, carabiners, and so on.)*

URBAN

STEP 2 - GETTING HOOKED
Alter Resource 9 to reflect the drugs that are popular in your city.

While alcohol is the most popular gateway drug in our *country*, some *cities* recognize that many teens are skipping alcohol completely and going straight to the more harmful drugs. Instead of starting with alcohol then moving onto marijuana and eventually harder drugs like crack cocaine, some city teens are getting their first highs from cocaine. If this is your situation, alter the reading of Resource 9 ("Everybody's Doing It," page 54) to reflect the drug which is most problematic in your community—alcohol may be the least of your problems. *(Needed: supplies listed in Step 2.)*

STEP 4 - DEAR CRABBY
Students write advice to teens.

"Dear Crabby" is a spin-off of the popular advice column "Dear Abbey"—but the writers who write "Dear Crabby" don't want help with the problem; they're writing just to voice their opinions and to be crabby. As such, the challenge is to give advice which has the best chance to get "crabby" teens to respond responsibly. Read the letters below. Students can respond by writing out their advice in the form of a newspaper column or simply stating it verbally to you.
• CRABBY #1: When I go to parties I get drunk off of beer with my friends. But my youth group is always dissin' my drinking. I don't see anything wrong since Jesus turned water to wine. Why should I stop?
• CRABBY #2: I'm no loser if I take a drink so not to offend those givin' it. Yeah, so what if I go to church? The rest of the people at church are just like me. Jesus hung with sinners too. Why should I stop?
• CRABBY #3: I've given up trying to walk focused with God. Some people are cut out for that. But as long as I go to church after a party, it all cancels out. Why should I stop? *(Needed: pens and paper or newsprint and markers.)*

OPTIONS

SESSION THREE

COMBINED

STEP 2 - DARE TO COMPARE
Compare junior highers' answers with senior highers'.

Step 2 asks students to discuss what a realistic encounter with drugs might look like at their schools or with their friends. Junior and senior high students, of course, come from different worlds. Use this option to help the two groups learn from one another. First ask for the junior highers to share their answers to the discussion questions in Step 2; write these answers on the left side of a whiteboard. Then ask the senior highers for their answers; write these answers on the right side of a white board. Add these questions: **Based on these answers, what are some of the differences between junior high and senior high? Junior highers, what did you learn about life in high school? Senior highers, what did you learn or remember about life in junior high?** *(Needed: whiteboard, marker.)*

STEP 3 - ALL CAN ANSWER
Broaden discussion questions to topics more general than drugs and alcohol.

Modify Step 3 to make the groups more applicable to students (especially young or somewhat sheltered junior highers) who have not been that close to tempting situations involving drugs and alcohol. For Group 1, have students write down a way that God provided a "way out" of any tempting situation—whether or not it specifically dealt with drugs and alcohol. For Group 2, have students write letters that ask for God's power in the area of their lives they need it most—whether or not it specifically has to do with drugs or alcohol. *(Needed: supplies listed in Step 3.)*

EXTRA CHALLENGE

STEP 3 - COUNT ON TRIALS
Study the persecution of the early Church.

In addition to or in place of the Bible study in Step 3, assign students to read John 16:33, Acts 14:21-22, Romans 5:3-5, Mark 4:17, Romans 8:35-39, Galatians 6:11-12, Acts 20:22-24, 2 Corinthians 6:3-10, and Colossians 1:24-26. Discuss: **Why do you think early believers went through so much persecution and affliction? Is it reasonable for us to assume that we may face similar situations? Why? How do most Christians today think and feel about suffering and being persecuted for God? How could these verses help remind us, even encourage us, to stand strong for God and say no to drugs and alcohol even if it means being persecuted?** Conclude your study by saying something like: **In North America, most of us want a painless Christianity. We want the best of both worlds: a godly walk and the closeness with worldly friends. That's not always possible and there are times you will have to draw the line. You will have to choose to take your stand, even if that means some friends reject you.** *(Needed: Bibles.)*

STEP 5 - WILL YOU LIVE FOR HIM?
Commit to live for Jesus Christ.

Read Romans 8:35-39. Ask: **What are you willing to die for?** Don't be surprised if many teens say they would die for God because it's the "right" answer. But don't be afraid to push your students further. **If we say we're willing to die for God, why do we have such a hard time living for Him?** Write the following on a chalkboard or piece of newsprint: He died for me. _____ will live for Him. Challenge students to write their name in the blank as a symbol of commitment in front of their peers. *(Needed: chalkboard or newsprint and marker.)*

PLANNING CHECKLIST

STEP 1 (5-10 MIN. UNLESS NOTED)
- ☐ **Extra Action:** No Quick Fixes
- ☐ **Small Group:** Quick Fix Storm
- ☐ **Large Group:** Problem Pictionary
- ☐ **Mostly Guys:** Miracle Products
- ☐ **Media:** Fix-All Commercials
- ☐ **Short Time:** Is *Just Say No* Enough? (3-5 min.)

STEP 2 (10-15 MIN. UNLESS NOTED)
- ☐ **Fellowship & Worship:** One on One
- ☐ **Mostly Girls:** Oprah Sin-Free
- ☐ **Urban:** Getting Hooked
- ☐ **Combined:** Dare to Compare

STEP 3 (15-20 MIN. UNLESS NOTED)
- ☐ **Large Group:** Tag-Team Teaching
- ☐ **Heard It All:** They Write the Study
- ☐ **Little Bible:** Jesus' Temptation
- ☐ **Mostly Guys:** Temptation Group
- ☐ **Short Time:** Power Packet (10-15 min.)
- ☐ **Combined:** All Can Answer
- ☐ **Extra Challenge:** Count on Trials

STEP 4 (10-15 MIN. UNLESS NOTED)
- ☐ **Small Group:** Search Engine
- ☐ **Heard It All:** Internet Threads
- ☐ **Extra Fun:** You Could . . . Laugh
- ☐ **Media:** Dear Mom and Dad
- ☐ **Urban:** Dear Crabby

STEP 5 (5-10 MIN. UNLESS NOTED)
- ☐ **Extra Action:** Prayer Stones
- ☐ **Little Bible:** Forgiveness Discussion
- ☐ **Fellowship & Worship:** Encouraged by Prayer
- ☐ **Mostly Girls** Questions in a Hat
- ☐ **Extra Fun:** T-Shirts
- ☐ **Extra Challenge:** Will You Live for Him?

SESSION 4
Glazed Eyes, Hangovers, and, uh... Really Great Prayer Times

YOUR GOALS FOR THIS SESSION:
Choose one or more

- ☐ To help students realize that use of drugs and alcohol hinder their spiritual walks.

- ☐ To help students understand that a Christian's body is the temple of the Holy Spirit.

- ☐ To challenge students to take the Drug Free Challenge—a commitment to honor their bodies as temples of the Holy Spirit, in particular by staying off alcohol, cigarettes, and narcotic drugs.

- ☐ Other: _____

Your Bible Base:

1 Corinthians 6:19-20
Ephesians 1:13-14

STEP 1

Drug Runners

In "Drug Runners," a variation of the popular party game "Runners," teams race to list as many kinds of drugs as they can: 10 minutes.
Or, choose one of the option categories highlighted in the left sidebar and see pages 73-77 for more "Getting Together" options.

OPTIONS

- LARGE GROUP
- MOSTLY GIRLS
- EXTRA FUN
- SHORT MEETING TIME
- URBAN

Supplies needed: blindfolds, obstacles (tables, chairs, etc.)
Set up: Set up your classroom or another room as a simple obstacle course. Break your students into pairs and hand out one blindfold to each team.

Give teams two minutes to come up with a team name and decide who will fill the following roles of either the Runner or Director. Explain to your students that their goal is to work together to plan a strategy to make it through the obstacle course. After you give them a couple of minutes to strategize, instruct the Directors to blindfold the Runners. This now leaves only the Director's voice to guide the Runner. But, tell the groups that once the Runner starts on the course, no one is allowed to touch him or her. All directions must be given orally. In addition, if a Runner touches an obstacle on the course, he or she is out and must leave the course. Of course, if several teams are doing the course at the same time, there will be several conflicting voices making it harder for the Runner to do what their Director says!

After a few tries, see how many groups were able to execute their plans to make it through the course successfully. Even if some of the pairs still aren't finished, end the game and bring the group back together. Interview a couple of Runners with questions like the following:

What was the best part of being a Runner?
How did you listen to your Director?
How did things change once you put the blindfold on?
Now interview a couple of Directors.
How did you like being in control?
Was it easy or hard to direct another person?
How were you able to avoid the obstacles?

Conclude by saying: **Obviously, we all face things that hinder us in life. Some things are put in our way. Other things we put in our own way! Drugs and alcohol can be like this. As your pair found out, life may be hard enough without all the obstacles we put in our bodies that hinder us! God's way is better.**

SESSION FOUR

STEP 2

Human Graffiti

Below, students "graffiti" on a body outline to symbolize physical effects of drugs: 10-15 minutes.
Or, choose one of the option categories highlighted in the right sidebar and see pages 73-77 for more "Getting Thirsty" options.

Supplies needed: newsprint or butcher paper, markers, copies of Resource 12, "Drug Info Sheet" (pages 69-70).
Set up: Prepare a body outline on newsprint before class. Have an adult or teen lay down on a long piece of newsprint or butcher paper and trace his or her outline onto the paper with a marker. Tape this outline to a wall in your room. It should be in a place where all students can see it. Hand out copies of Resource 12.

Resource 12 contains some facts primarily about the physical effects of drugs and alcohol. This is information students have probably heard before in one form or another. It's important, though, that students *interact* with this information. For the "Human Graffiti," students will draw symbols of the physical effects of drugs on a newsprint outline of a human body.

To start the activity, choose volunteers to take turns reading one section at a time from Resource 12. Allow the readers to symbolize the physical effects of the drug or drugs discussed by making marks, words, or "graffiti" of some sort on the newsprint outline. For example, if a student reads that "Marijuana can cause lung damage, impair mental skills, and cause an acute panic or anxiety reaction," the reader might then mark red X's or other graffiti where the lungs, brain, and other affected parts of the body on the figure outline. The more disorderly the markings, the better. Not all the information on Resource 12 translates easily to a specific place to "graffiti," but in such cases you can discuss the psychological and spiritual effects. When you get done reading Resource 12, your newsprint figure should be significantly "vandalized."

Discuss: **How good does the human body look after drugs and alcohol have gotten a hold of it? Do you want your body to look something like this? What is the purpose of our bodies? Are we to drive them hard and fast until we die, or are we to take care of them? Do drugs and alcohol help us do that?**

OPTIONS

- EXTRA ACTION
- FELLOWSHIP & WORSHIP
- MOSTLY GIRLS
- MOSTLY GUYS
- MEDIA
- JR. HIGH / HIGH SCHOOL COMBINED

CUSTOM CURRICULUM

STEP 3

Who, Me a Temple?

Students will discuss what it means to be temples of the Holy Spirit: 15-20 minutes.
Or, choose one of the option categories highlighted in the left sidebar and see pages 73-77 for more "Getting the Word" options.

OPTIONS
- SMALL GROUP
- LARGE GROUP
- LITTLE BIBLE BACKGROUND
- EXTRA FUN
- URBAN
- EXTRA CHALLENGE

Supplies needed: Bibles.

Students should have a pretty good reminder in front of them of the physical effects of using drugs and alcohol. Now it's time to talk about the spiritual consequences. Choose students to read 1 Corinthians 6:19-20 (even though these verses come from a passage specifically dealing with sexual sin, the principle can appropriately be applied to drug and alcohol use) and Ephesians 1:13-14.

What does it mean that Christians are "temples of the Holy Spirit"? (God lives inside us in the person of the Holy Spirit.)

Why does God choose to have the Holy Spirit live in us? (He gives us the Holy Spirit to help us in the ways that Jesus helped the disciples when He was with them on earth.)

What does the Holy Spirit do for us? (Guides us into God's truth; gives us power to do God's work on earth; convicts us of sin.)

What does it mean to be a "temple"? (A temple is a dwelling place.)

So what does it mean that our bodies are "temples of the Holy Spirit"? (God's spirit lives in us constantly. We are the dwelling place of the Holy Spirit.)

So let's make the connection. Drugs and alcohol and the temple of the Holy Spirit. What can we learn from the passages we've just read?

Since we are temples of the Holy Spirit, what difference should that make in the way we treat our bodies?

Look at the newsprint poster up here. Imagine for a moment that you are God. Imagine this newsprint poster was the actual body of a Christian—imagine it was the dwelling place of the Holy Spirit that you have sent to help your children. How do you think you might feel about seeing such damage to this body?

The Bible says your body is the Temple of the Holy Spirit. That means when you take drugs into your body, you bring the Holy Spirit along with you. Would you take a six pack into church and drink it during the sermon? Would you snort cocaine during worship? Then why would you put drugs into your body when you know that God values you and your body this much?

Temples of the Holy Spirit
I Corinthians 6:19-20

- ◆ BACKGROUND BYTES: In Old Testament times, the temple was though of as God's "home." Of course, God revealed Himself (often through His Holy Spirit) when and where He wanted. But the temple did have immense importance as the place where believers worshiped God, and as such it was treated with the utmost respect.
- ◆ SCRIPTURE BYTES: In Old Testament times, the Holy Spirit was "in" certain people (Genesis 41:38; Daniel 5:11:14) and "came upon" certain others (Judges 14:19 and 6:34, I Samuel 10:9-11 and 16:13). But His ministry was limited. Now, God has chosen to live in all believers in the person of the Holy Spirit (Ephesians 1:13-14). Students can know the Holy Spirit lives in them and works in them when they experience, among other things, the conviction of sin (John 16:8-11) and the filling of the Spirit (or God empowering them to live Christ's life through them).
- ◆ BYTE-SIZE INSIGHTS: Help Christian students be convinced that the Holy Spirit lives in them by reviewing as specifically as you can your own experiences with the Holy Spirit with them—in other words, teach them exactly what it means to experience the Spirit's conviction, forgiveness, and leading. The most important thing students can take from this lesson is a firm resolve to honor God with their bodies since He values them so much to make them a dwelling place for His Spirit.

CUSTOM CURRICULUM

STEP 4

Testimonials

Below, students listen to the testimonies of two former drug and/or alcohol users who have seen God work in their lives: 10-15 minutes.
Or, choose one of the option categories highlighted in the right sidebar and see pages 73-77 for more "Getting the Point" options.

Set up: You will need to recruit two mature teens or young adults who are willing to talk about their past experiences with drugs and alcohol.

Your guest speakers can give their testimonials in one of two formats.

• If your speakers are not experienced talking to teens, they may need some help telling their stories. You would do well to interview your guests. Know their stories ahead of time. Ask questions that will help them, such as: **When did you first start using drugs? How did that affect you physically? How about spiritually? What happened then?** If possible, prepare them with a list of the questions you will ask ahead of time.

• Or, you may choose to get the students involved in a question and answer format. Guests should give their testimony in a "nutshell" form and then field questions from your students. Use this second format only if you're confident that your group will show interest and ask plenty of questions of your guest speakers. Be prepared with questions of your own, just in case.

Regardless of the format you use, look for speakers that get beyond cliches. You want real people talking to real people. This is a great opportunity for students to hear some of the spiritual effects that drugs and alcohol can have on a person. Pray for your speakers and support them as they talk to your students.

SESSION FOUR

STEP 5

The Drug Free Challenge

Below, students sign a Drug Free Certificate or Commitment Card. Or, choose one of the options in the right sidebar and see pages 73-77 for more "Getting Personal" options.

OPTIONS

Supplies needed: cut-out copies of Resource 13 (page 71), pens.

Students who take the Drug Free Challenge make a commitment to abstain from certain drugs and alcohol. Think through how you want to present this challenge. We encourage you to challenge your group to abstain from alcohol, cigarettes/tobacco, and narcotic drugs (like methamphetamines, cocaine, and marijuana). Have students write out their commitments in their own words and include only the specific things they are ready to commit to.

Optional: On Resource 13, we've included both a Drug Free Certificate and a Commitment Card. Use whichever you think will work with your students. To prepare the Certificate, copy it onto heavy, formal-looking stock paper and cut it out. There is one line for students' own signature and three for whichever accountability partners they wish to include—parents, peers, youth leaders, and so on. To prepare the Commitment Card, copy the boxes at the bottom of the resource on heavy or regular paper and cut them out. There is less room for students' own words, but the cards are small enough that students can keep them in their wallets or purses.

To lead your students through their commitments, tell them the commitment you're making. Next, give students a chance to complete their sheets. Make sure no one feels pressured to make a commitment. Before closing, allow volunteers to share what they wrote.

Close your time by praying that God will give your students the power they need to honor their commitments.

Note: Many students may need a trusted adult to talk and walk with through their decisions. They will need an adult's wisdom, support, and encouragement. Be willing and ready to support them in their commitments.

THE DRUG FREE CHALLENGE
Drug Info Sheet

RESOURCE 12

Marijuana is not a "hard" drug like cocaine. I can't get addicted.

Is this "hard" enough? Consider the facts: marijuana will damage your lungs, impair your brain's ability to think like a normal person, may cause a severe panic or anxiety reaction, and can lead to severe problems with your hormones, especially for teenagers. What's more, marijuana almost never stops with marijuana. It's called a "gateway" drug because it often leads to use of even more dangerous drugs. Thousands of teens in North America ARE addicted to marijuana.

It's my body. If I feel like smoking, I'll smoke. If I want to drink, I'll drink.

If you smoke, you slowly destroy your lungs, your teeth, and your ability to function without nicotine. Over 10 thousand people die of lung cancer related to smoking every year. If you drink excessive amounts, you'll destroy your liver, kill brain cells, and risk becoming an alcoholic.

Smoking cigarettes helps me relax.

Nicotine, the active drug in cigarettes, doesn't help the normal body relax. In fact, it gives healthy bodies a quick rush. But when your body gets used to the rush caused by nicotine, it starts to depend on it. It gets to the point where you can't relax without nicotine.

"I took some pills at a party one time. I think they were amphetamines. It was a pretty cool high. Nothing bad happened to me. I don't see what the big deal is. I'll probably try it again."

If you start messing around with amphetamines or other "uppers," it's not a matter of if something bad will to your body but when. Prolonged use can cause headaches, blurred vision, dizziness, sleeplessness, and anxiety. An amphetamine injection creates a sudden increase in blood pressure that can cause death from stroke, very high fever, or heart failure. Over a long period of time, you'll probably suffer from hallucinations and paranoia. Long-term use may also lead to malnutrition, skin disorders, ulcers, and various diseases that come with vitamin deficiencies.

I drink because everybody else does. It's how we "party." It's how we celebrate.

Aren't there better ways to celebrate than by killing brain cells, damaging sexual organs, causing possible hangovers, sacrificing your integrity if you can't be honest with your parents, friends, and others, and risking the possibility that you might get so into "partying" that it will rob your energy for other pursuits?

I know cocaine and crack are dangerous. But that's a risk I'm willing to take. I like the high too much to stop.

Enjoy the high while it lasts because you're heading for some low spots if you don't stop, including: confusion, slurred speech, anxiety, serious psychological problems—like the inability to function in school or hold down a normal job!

I'll never get addicted. I know what I can handle.

Be careful how much you trust yourself. It starts like this: you start liking the high you get from a drug, then you start needing it, then you find that you need something stronger to get a high, then before you know it—before you've ever planned for it to happen—you're fully addicted. It's a physical fact. No one is immune. Every single time you take a hard drug you risk addiction.

It's not a sin to drink if you don't get drunk.

There's a huge difference between asking "Is it a sin?" and "What will honor God?" What are your motives for drinking?

THE DRUG FREE CHALLENGE

RESOURCE 13

I will honor God with what I put in my body.

I will honor my body because it is the temple of the Holy Spirit.

I will:

_____   _____

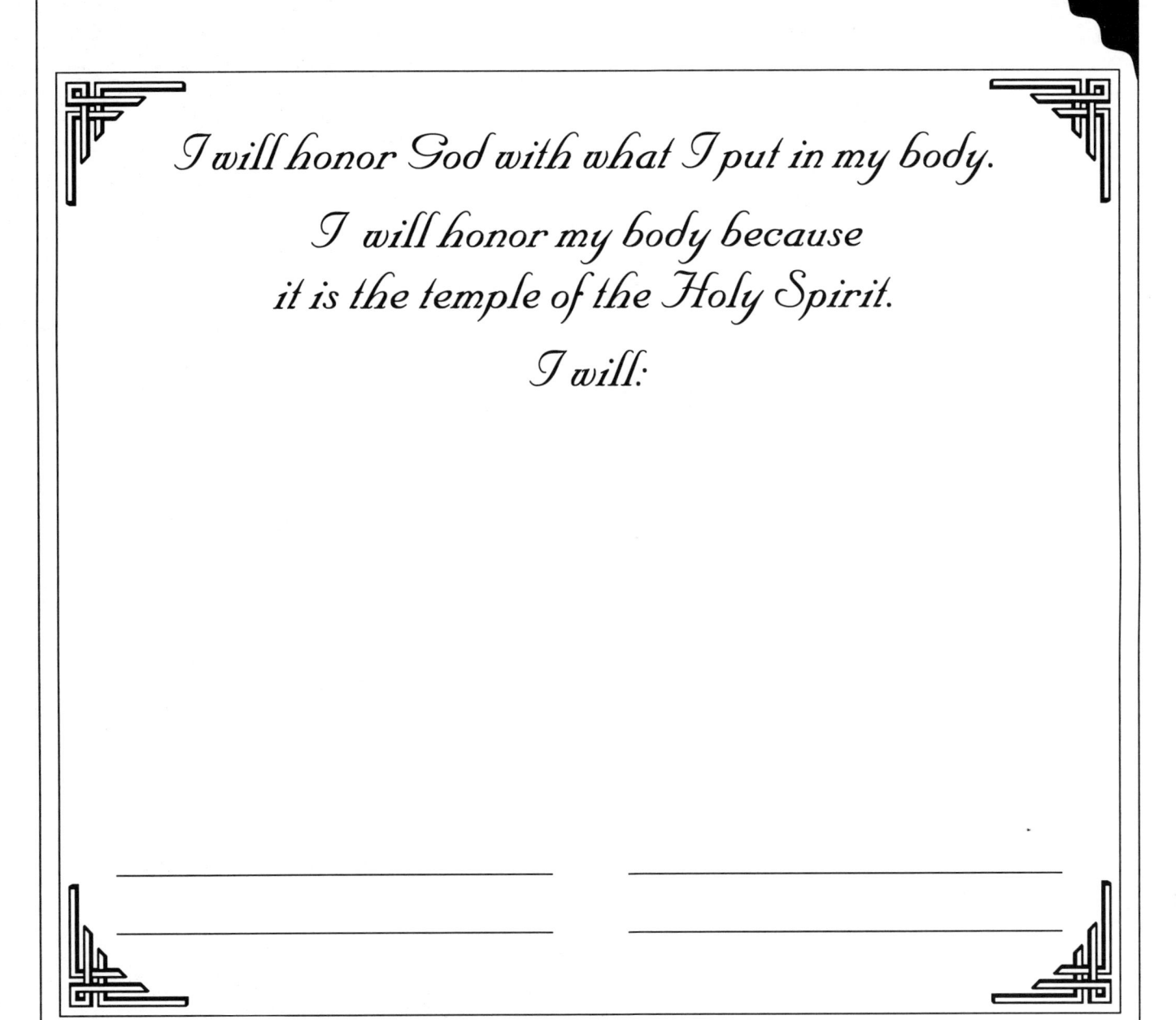

My **BODY** is God's temple. I will honor God with what I put in my body.

_____
Your Signature

1 CORINTHIANS 6:19, 20

I will:

OPTIONS

S E S S I O N   F O U R

EXTRA ACTION

STEP 2 - THEY DON'T MIX!
Match stimuli with responses and discuss why drugs and Christianity don't mix.

Put this list of "stimuli" on slips of white paper: back rub, headache, hug, drinking coffee, skydiving. Put this list of responses on slips of colored paper: relaxation, irritability, closeness, sleepiness, arousal, hyperactivity, exhilaration. Give each student one of slip of paper. (Discard what you don't need or duplicate some items on the list if you need more.) Tell students to find their match—the stimulus that produces the response on their card, or vice versa. Answers are somewhat subjective. Congratulate the winners—the two students who connected first. **Can a headache cause relaxation? Can skydiving make you feel sleepy (while you're diving, not after)? Of course not! Certain things you do to your body cause certain emotional and even spiritual responses. What kind of physical responses do drugs cause? But what about spiritual responses? When you take drugs, you take control of your body out of the hands of God and put it in the hands of a substance.** *(Needed: slips of white and colored paper, pen.)*

STEP 5 - TAKE A STAND
Students are challenged to stand up together to symbolize commitments.

Use Step 5 as directed. Then tell students to partner up. Have partners sit on the floor back to back. Partners should explain their commitments to each other. Then tell them to: cross their arms in front of their chest and push against each other to stand up. Once they have made it successfully (no using hands; no locking arms) they should remain standing and pray for each other's commitment. Use this activity as a final reminder that when students "take a stand" it is important to "lean on" each other. *(Needed: supplies listed in Step 5.)*

SMALL GROUP

STEP 3 - TEMPLE TRIP
Visit a sanctuary or worship center.

With a small group, you have a great opportunity to do location events. Not only are these location options visually effective, they also provide a sense of adventure and an element of excitement for your group. After you do the "human graffiti" project in Step 2, take your students on a walk to your sanctuary or worship center. When you arrive, discuss: **What is the purpose of this worship center? (It's a place to worship God, learn about God and His Word, be with other Christians, etc.) Why do you think so much time is spent keeping our worship center clean? Why do you think people try to behave better sometimes when they come here? What would we communicate if we didn't keep this place clean or we didn't act respectfully in it?** Study the Scripture as directed in Step 3 that says our bodies are temples of the Holy Spirit. Help students see why they should take care of and respect their bodies. If possible, stay in the worship center to end your lesson.

STEP 5 - COMMITMENT POSTER
Make a poster that includes all the commitment sheets.

In a small group, you can be creative with how you facilitate additional accountability. Use Step 5 as directed. Then have students help you design a large poster—this can be as simple as putting a title like "Taking a Stand," "Taking the Challenge" or "The Drug Free Challenge" on top of a large sheet of posterboard. Encourage students to tape or glue their commitment cards to the poster. Remind students that doing this means that many people (other students, pastor, parents) will know they have made this commitment. *(Needed: newsprint, commitment sheets from Step 5.)*

LARGE GROUP

STEP 1 - BEER JINGLES
See how well groups do remembering songs from beer commercials.

Say: **Your challenge is to think up more jingles or slogans from beer or alcohol commercials than the other team can.** Give teams 45 seconds to brainstorm, then start by asking the girls to sing a jingle or yell out a slogan. The guys must respond with a different jingle or slogan. No jingle may be repeated during the game. When one team fails to come up with a new song or slogan in 15 seconds, the other team wins. Use this activity to discuss the prevalence of alcohol in our culture. What does it say about our culture when we can remember so many alcohol ads? What does it say about how lightly our culture views alcohol?

STEP 3 - REALLY HUMAN GRAFFITI
Use Step 3, but take the phrase "human graffiti" literally.

The "Human Graffiti" idea may not get all your students involved. But this idea at least will give them something fun to watch and listen to. Choose one student or adult you know will have a good sense of humor and play along with the "human graffiti" activity—or, if you're really brave, play the following role yourself. When students volunteer to read from the "Drug Info Sheet" (Resource 12), supply them with whip cream, shaving cream, silly string, or something else fun and messy and let them "graffiti" your human volunteer at an appropriate place on his or her body. The discussion questions at the end of Step 3 should take on new meaning after this activity. *(Needed: shaving cream or other, other supplies listed in Step 3.)*

OPTIONS

SESSION FOUR

HEARD IT ALL BEFORE

STEP 4 - MY B-O-O-RING LIFE
Two testimony options.

Many kids who have grown up in the church feel that a life without drugs, drunkenness, and mayhem somehow disqualifies them from having an effective testimony. Here are two possible ways to deal with this distorted sense of inferiority. Arrange for and include one testimony from someone who has consistently resisted the temptation to become involved in this lifestyle and allow this person to speak from a positive perspective about God's grace and protection and the lack of regret they now enjoy. Another way to make the same point would be to take the role of "devil's advocate" and engage your guests in a dialogue where you talk about how much you wished that you had a story like theirs so that you could share a powerful testimony like the one just given. Your guests will undoubtedly make a strong case for purity which will speak loudly to kids.

STEP 5 - BEWARE "JUST BEHAVIOR"
Discuss deeper issues with students.

Making a "Drug Free Commitment" is measurable and concrete. But remember that drug and alcohol use is often merely a symptom of deeper issues. Be wary of stressing the behavior of saying no to drugs and alcohol in this session—and this series—without addressing some deeper issues. Encourage students to include when they write out their commitments other, less measurable ways to honor God with their bodies and their lives: I will get to know God more deeply, I will make wise choices about friends, and so on. You might be surprised how many of them live with their own struggles on a daily basis. *(Needed: see supplies listed in Step 5.)*

LITTLE BIBLE BACKGROUND

STEP 3 - BUT JESUS DID IT!
Discuss Jesus turning water into wine.

Be prepared to answer students' questions about the use of wine in the Bible. Group members may point out that Jesus changed water into wine at a party (see John 2:1-11). The Bible Bytes box on page 66 does a good job pointing out that Bible condones the use of a *little* wine (1 Timothy 5:23) but doesn't condone drunkenness (Ephesians 5:18). Emphasize that the Bible certainly commands us to obey the laws of the land—and your students break the law if they drink.

STEP 4 - SIN OR SICKNESS?
Be prepared to discuss this issue.

During the testimonials, one or both of your guests may refer to drug addiction or alcohol abuse as either a sin or a sickness. If substance abuse is a sickness, then it should be taken to a doctor to be cured. If substance abuse is a sin, then it should be taken to the Great Physician. Substance abuse is fundamentally a sin that can rapidly progress into a sickness. In addition to the physical and mental effects already discussed, drug abuse can also have a terrible and unexpected impact on the spirit, including guilt, despair, pain, and suffering.

FELLOWSHIP & WORSHIP

STEP 2 - ALL ABOARD!
Groups get closer by answering questions.

Sometimes activity can be a great way to encourage fellowship among your students. Divide your group into teams of four or five. You will need one 2' x 2' wooden platform for each team (a sheet of 1/2" plywood stabilized on 2' x 4's works well; if all else fails, this activity will still work with pieces of flat cardboard). Place the platforms in a circle. Each team must squeeze and fit on the platform, then answer the first question together. Then two volunteers must leave and move counterclockwise to the next platform. Teams answer the next question while huddled tightly together, then two students who did not move the first time must rotate for the third question, and so on. *(Needed: wood platform, plywood and 2 x 4's, or 2' x 2' sheets of cardboard.)*

STEP 4 - PRAYER TESTIMONIAL
A "prayer testimonial" is a testimony with prayer woven through it.

Ask several adults or students to share about their past or present struggles with drug or alcohol use. Ask them to outline their testimony in four parts: what they feel led them to experiment with drugs or alcohol in the first place; how it effected their life; what caused/enabled them to stop; and, what lessons they learned. After each section of the testimony, have the person sharing pause and lead your students in a short time of prayer, focusing on what was just shared.

OPTIONS

SESSION FOUR

MOSTLY GIRLS

STEP 1 - WHAT ABOUT DIET PILLS?
Discuss diet pills.

As the girls list various drugs, don't forget that diet drugs are also frequently misused by adolescent girls. Discuss: **Are diet pills drugs? What kind of side effects do they have? Should Christians use diet pills?**

STEP 2 - GLAM SCAM
Evaluate the messages of magazines marketed to teen girls.

Bring in a couple of fashion magazines that your students are reading (*Vogue, Mademoiselle*, and so on.) Have students browse through and pull out pictures and articles that run contrary to the idea of our bodies being the temple of the Holy Spirit. There may be articles on unhealthy diet plans (for example, eat nothing but grapefruit seeds and cheese curds for a month), pictures of ultra-thin models, or advice columns on how to drink and not get sick. Then have them go through the same magazines looking for pictures/articles that run complimentary to the idea that we need to take care of our bodies. Discuss: **Which set of articles/photos is larger? Why is that? Is the trend towards one direction or the other? What are some of the short-term effects of abusing our bodies? What are some of the long-term effects?** (Needed: magazines, scissors.)

MOSTLY GUYS

STEP 2 - MANLY TEMPLES
Help guys see that it is more "manly" to honor God than use drugs.

Your guys want and need to know that being a temple of the Holy Spirit is more manly than using drugs. Use the directions for Step 2 with these variations. When you make the newsprint outline, make it large, manly, and muscular. Cut the heads of a few muscle men out of muscle magazines and let your guys pick one and glue it to the top of the body outline. (The head will be smaller than the body but that will make it funny.) Before using Resource 13, discuss: **What does it mean to be manly?** Whatever words students come up with, write them on the body outline. **Why do some people think it's "manly" to use drugs?** When you use Resource 13, ask students if destroying your body has anything to do with being courageous, strong, powerful, or anything else they used to describe manliness. Encourage them by helping them see that when they take care of and build their bodies they honor and glorify God. (Needed: muscle magazines, scissors, tape, marker, other supplies listed in Step 3.)

STEP 4 - GUY-FRIENDLY SPEAKERS
Address specific guy issues.

There are a number of things you can do to make the testimonies "guy friendly." First, choose male speakers. Also, prepare your speakers to talk about their experiences with wanting to fit in with other guys, needing to look cool and tough, the way that guys often enjoy and even crave physical "highs," and so on. In addition to the discussion questions listed in Step 4, ask your speakers: **Was taking drugs a way to impress your friends? Why do guys want so badly to impress other guys? What would you say to someone today who thinks using drugs or alcohol is part of "being a man?"**

EXTRA FUN

STEP 1 - REAL FUN
Ideas for starting the meeting off on a fun note.

Drugs are fake fun. They give fake solutions, fake confidence, fake emotions, and fake wisdom. No one is really more fun, braver, cuter, or more brilliant because of drugs. Just the opposite is true. Drugs stunt the real growth and fun of a person. So to emphasize the point that Christians walking in the Holy Spirit have more fun than people who anesthetize their minds, how about blowing out of the classroom and having some real fun (or staying in the class and throwing a party). Go play a game in a park, chow down on ice cream, have a joke-telling session (come prepared with some great jokes). Do something you know your students will enjoy. When you are done, point out that the end result of drugs is the *dulling* of fun, diminishing of imagination, and dampening of personality.

STEP 3 - YOU BROUGHT WHAT?
Bring limburger cheese into the House of the Lord to make a point.

Put limburger cheese in a plastic, sealable bag. Seal it and bring it to class out of sight. When you begin to discuss the idea that Christians bodies should be treated with respect as temples where God dwells, quietly drag out the cheese and undo the seal on the bag. The aroma will no doubt have an instant effect. Say things like: "Hey, I don't mind . . . It's not hurting anyone . . . I don't do this very often . . ." and other things teens say to justify why they bring stuff that stinks (such as drugs) into God's temple (their bodies.). (Needed: limburger cheese, baggie.)

OPTIONS

SESSION FOUR

MEDIA

STEP 2 - DRUGS ON TV
Show quick clips of drug use.

Introduce the discussion by showing a number of clips of drug use. Ahead of time, prepare a 2-5 minute video including clips from TV shows and movies, and still-life shots from magazines of people discussing and using drugs.
(Needed: video camera, videotape, TV, VCR.)

STEP 4 - VIDEO TESTIMONIES
Tape a teen' or parents' testimonies.

A testimony on video can either compliment or replace your "live" testimonies. Two ideas: 1) Go to a drug rehab center and ask for permission to interview a recovering teenager. For added effect, include clips of the hospital entrance, walls, and waiting room. 2) Interview students' parents talking honestly about their stories of drug and alcohol use. NOTE: For tips on filming interviews, see page 28. *(Needed: video camera, videotape, TV, VCR.)*

SHORT MEETING TIME

STEP 1 - ONE LONG LIST
Brainstorm a list of all kinds of drugs.

Begin brainstorming a list of all the kinds of drugs students can think of. Write a list on the a piece of newsprint. Use the discussion questions at the end of Step 1. Or, remember that if you're really pressed for time you can skip Step 1. If your group is conditioned to dive right into the meeting, you can usually start the session with Step 2 and not miss out on much "meat." *(Needed: newsprint, marker.)*

STEP 4 - QUICK TESTIMONIES
Prepare speakers to be brief.

Prepare your speakers to give their testimonies in one minute or less. This way they can hit the high points and be available for questions afterwards. If you don't have time to find speakers, give your own testimony, whether you used drugs in the past or didn't.

STEP 5 - TAKE IT HOME

Briefly explain how students may use Resource 13, then send it home with them. This will give them a chance to think about their commitments. Give students a chance to share next week. *(Needed: cut-out copies of Resource 13.)*

URBAN

STEP 1 - IS MARIJUANA A DRUG?
Give this prevalent drug extra attention.

Marijuana, particularly amongst the Rasta, hip hop, and punk youth cultures, is not considered a drug, but just a "stronger cigarette." Discuss: **Is marijuana a drug? Why or why not?** Since many church teens will give the answer they believe you want, split them into two groups and ask that each group create a defense as to "why" or "why it is not" a real (or hard) drug. Let the debate begin. After, to show the acceptance of marijuana in our culture as a friendly not harmful drug, ask them to list every nickname they can think of, for example: MJ, Bo, Mary Jane, Buddha, Indo, Budd, Refa, Blunt, and Weed.

STEP 3 - HIGH IN WHICH SPIRIT?
Discuss meanings of "spiritual high."

A number of Pentecostal and Holiness churches use the phrase "Get high in the Spirit." Use Step 3 as written, then teach students that there are two kinds of getting high in the spiritual universe. 1) The Greek word "pharmakia" is sometimes translated as "witchcraft" and often refers to a destructive pseudo-spiritual high generated by Satan via physical drug use and abuse (Galatians 5:20; Deuteronomy 18:10-12, 1 Samuel 15:23, Exodus 22:18). 2) The Greek word "paraclete" on the other hand is translated "Holy Spirit" which refers to a constructive spiritual high which gives comfort and power in a personal relationship with Jesus Christ (Acts 2:1-21; John 14:16,26; 15:26; 16:7). Teach students that the first-century church saw drug involvement as witchcraft which comes from the Greek root we use as pharmacy or pharmacist. To conclude, ask students to compare and discuss how inadequate a witchcraft high is compared to the Holy Spirit high, like the one received in the second chapter of Acts.

OPTIONS

SESSION FOUR

COMBINED

STEP 2 - MAKE THE CALL
Students "make the call" about some controversial situations.

Read each of the following four statements one at a time: **All drugs should always be avoided; Alcohol is a drug; Tobacco is a drug; Drugs will never mess me up—I can handle it.** After each statement, ask your students to stand at the left side of your room if they agree with the statement or the right side of the room if they disagree. Ask some students to explain why they stood where they did.

STEP 4 - UP CLOSE AND PERSONAL
Students interview your guest speakers in small groups.

Instead of interviewing the guest speakers yourself, ask students themselves to get up close and personal with the guests. This will both help students get more actively involved with the testimonies and help avoid either silence or potentially random questions from junior highers. Choose two students (one senior higher and one junior higher) ahead of time and ask them to come to your meeting 30 minutes early so they can meet with you and the two people giving the testimonials. Pair up one student with each guest speaker. Explain that the student will be interviewing the guest speaker. Help the student develop 3-4 questions that the student can ask during Step 4. Make sure that the students and guest speakers are clear on the questions before you begin the session.

EXTRA CHALLENGE

STEP 3 - JUST "ONE LITTLE HIT"
Spend extra time studying temptation.

Use Step 3 as directed. Then break into three groups and assign each one of the following passages: Judges 16; 2 Samuel 11; Acts 8:9-23; Acts 4:32—5:11. Instruct groups to report back to class on these questions: **What "one little hit" was your character(s) tempted to take? How did he (they) give in to the temptation? What was the result?** After the presentations, conclude by saying: **Temptation to do drugs is just another tool the enemy uses in his attempt to turn our hearts and minds away from Christ.** *(Needed: supplies listed in Step 3.)*

STEP 4 - ROAD TRIP
Visit a halfway house.

If possible, make arrangements for your group to drive over to a local halfway house at the end of Step 3. Most halfway houses will allow visitors to come in and listen during group or Bible study time. Your students will see and hear first-hand the destructive end results that start with "just one little hit." If you can't go during the meeting, you might set up an alternate time. Once there, you may want to volunteer your time to help paint or complete some other project.

STEP 5 - RECOGNITION IDEAS
Recognize your students' commitments.

Consider these options as ways to honor your students' Drug Free Commitments.
• Hold a dinner banquet that honors students' commitments. Invite parents and friends. Let students take turns briefly explaining why they made commitments.
• Have your senior pastor sign the commitment sheets and/or recognize students at a Sunday morning service.
• Feature students in a church or youth group newsletter.

PLANNING CHECKLIST

STEP 1 (5-10 MIN. UNLESS NOTED)
❑ **Large Group**: Beer Jingles
❑ **Mostly Girls**: What about Diet Pills?
❑ **Extra Fun**: Real Fun
❑ **Short Time**: One Long List (3-5 min.)
❑ **Urban**: Is Marijuana a Drug?

STEP 2 (10-15 MIN. UNLESS NOTED)
❑ **Extra Action**: They Don't Mix!
❑ **Fellowship & Worship**: All Aboard!
❑ **Mostly Girls**: Glam Scam
❑ **Mostly Guys**: Manly Temples
❑ **Media**: Drugs on TV
❑ **Combined**: Make the Call

STEP 3 (15-20 MIN. UNLESS NOTED)
❑ **Small Group**: Temple Trip
❑ **Large Group**: *Really* Human Graffiti
❑ **Little Bible**: But Jesus Did It!
❑ **Extra Fun**: You Brought What?
❑ **Urban**: High in Which Spirit?
❑ **Extra Challenge**: Just "One Little Hit"

STEP 4 (10-15 MIN. UNLESS NOTED)
❑ **Heard It All**: My B-O-O-RING Life
❑ **Little Bible**: Sin or Sickness?
❑ **Fellowship & Worship**: Prayer Testimonial
❑ **Mostly Guys**: Guy-Friendly Speakers
❑ **Media**: Video Testimonies
❑ **Short Time**: Quick Testimonies
❑ **Combined**: Up Close and Personal
❑ **Extra Challenge**: Road Trip

STEP 5 (5-10 MIN. UNLESS NOTED)
❑ **Extra Action**: Take a Stand
❑ **Small Group**: Commitment Poster
❑ **Heard It All**: Beware "Just Behavior"
❑ **Short Time**: Take It Home
❑ **Extra Challenge**: Recognition Ideas

SESSION 5

Throwing the Life Preserver

YOUR GOALS FOR THIS SESSION:
Choose one or more

☐ To help students realize that they might be God's best tool to help their friends who struggle with drugs and alcohol.

☐ To help students understand basic intervention principles from the ministry of Jesus that will make a difference in the lives of their friends who struggle with drugs and alcohol.

☐ To provide students with practical strategies for helping their friends who abuse drugs and alcohol.

☐ Other: _____

Your Bible Base:

John 4:1-26, 39

STEP 1

Would You Rather . . .

Below, students step to one side of the room or the other to vote on which of two choices they'd rather say to their friends: 5-10 minutes.
Or, choose one of the option categories highlighted in the left sidebar and see pages 89-93 for more "Getting Together" options.

OPTIONS: Little Bible Background, Mostly Girls

Supplies needed: tape.
Set up: Place a long piece of tape down the middle of your room.

In today's youth culture, it's hard enough for teens to tell a friend his or her shoe is untied, much less confront a friend about drug and alcohol use. Relativity and tolerance are the highest values of the culture.

Explain to students that you will read two choices. They should decide which they'd rather do, then move to the appropriate side of the room. Read the choices below, one at a time. When you read the first of two choices, point to the left side of your room. When you read the second, point to the right side.

Would you rather tell your friend . . .
- "Your clothes don't match" or, "You didn't make the team"?
- "You made me angry" or, "You made a mistake"?
- "You have a drug problem" or, "I have a problem with the way you talk to me"?
- "You didn't make the school play" or, "You've got toilet paper stuck to your shoe."
- "Your crush asked someone else to homecoming" or, "What you said this morning made me mad."
- "You drank too much last Friday and made a fool of yourself" or, "I'm really concerned about you. I think you need to get some help with your drinking."
- "You're spending way too much time at the mall" or, "I've heard a rumor that you're doing drugs. Is it true?"

Discuss: **Is confronting your friends hard or easy? Why is confrontation so hard? What's the hardest thing to confront your friends on?**

SESSION FIVE

STEP 2

Advice Sharing

Below, students build relationship in small groups by sharing their thoughts about how to deal with a friend who uses drugs or alcohol: 10-15 minutes. Or, choose an option category highlighted in the right sidebar and see pages 89-93 for more "Getting Thirsty" options.

OPTIONS

- EXTRA ACTION
- FELLOWSHIP & WORSHIP
- EXTRA FUN
- MEDIA
- SHORT MEETING TIME
- URBAN

Supplies needed: index cards.
Set up: Make four or more sets of question cards by writing the questions listed below each on its own index card. Make sure to number each card. Divide into four or more groups (optimal size: three to six students). Give each group a second set of index cards numbered one through nine.

Students take turns choosing a numbered index card and then they answer the question card with the corresponding number (for example, if they choose a "6," they answer Question Card #6).

Questions:
1. On a scale of 1 to 10, how hard is it to stay drug free?
2. Share about a friend or someone you know who has struggled with drug or alcohol use in the past. (No names please.)
3. Do you ever fear that you might become drug dependent or an alcoholic? Why or why not?
4. What percentage of people who start trying drugs do you think get addicted to drugs? Why do you think some people are able to use drugs for a long period of time and not get addicted while others get addicted right away?
5. Do you believe relying on God alone can be enough to resist the temptation to experiment with drugs and alcohol?
6. Do you think people who are addicted to drugs and alcohol can just stop if they put their minds to it? Why or why not? If not, what do they have to do to overcome their problem?
7. On a scale of 1 to 10, how hard do you think it is to stop using drugs or alcohol once you start using them? Why?
8. Share about a time you confronted someone you knew who had a drug or alcohol problem. If you have never confronted a person with a drug or alcohol problem, tell why not.
9. Flash forward five years into the future. You never thought it would happen to you, but you find yourself with a serious drug problem. You know you're out of control but you feel like you can't tell anyone. Would you want your friends to confront you or leave you alone? Why? How would you want your friends to confront you?

CUSTOM CURRICULUM

STEP 3

What Would Jesus Do?

Below, students discover and discuss insights about how to confront people by reading about Jesus' encounter with the Samaritan woman: 15-20 minutes. Or, choose one of the option categories highlighted in the left sidebar and see pages 89-93 for more "Getting the Word" options.

Supplies needed: copies of Resource 14, "Insight Cards" (page 85), Bibles, pencils, chalkboard or whiteboard.
Set up: Pass out copies of Resource 14 and pencils. Break into three small groups.

Write these questions on the board: **What was Jesus' attitude towards her? How did He approach her? How did Jesus confront her? How did He follow up the challenge?** In small groups, students should read John 4:1-26, then write down on their "insight cards" any insights they learn from Jesus about how to help others with their problems. Wherever possible, students should try to produce insights that answer the questions above. When you come back together to discuss each group's answers, be prepared with the following insights of your own. Intersperse these into the conversation as needed.

What attitude did Jesus take towards her? (verses 7-9) Jesus accepted her for who she was and treated her with dignity and respect. Most Jewish men considered themselves above both Samaritans (who were half-Jews) and women. But Jesus saw past the Samaritan woman's labels and treated her the way she deserved to be treated.

How did He approach her? (verse 10) He initiated contact. He put Himself out there and was willing to get involved personally.

How did Jesus confront her? (verses 16-19) He waited until she was asking questions of Him. He didn't water down the truth. He spoke clearly and boldly. He challenged her to think differently.

How did He follow up the challenge? (verses 25-26) He helped her get past her problem and helped her experience a relationship with God. Even though this is just one conversation, Jesus gives us a clear example

OPTIONS:
SMALL GROUP
LARGE GROUP
HEARD IT ALL BEFORE
LITTLE BIBLE BACKGROUND
MEDIA
SHORT MEETING TIME
URBAN
JR. HIGH/HIGH SCHOOL COMBINED
EXTRA CHALLENGE

81

of how we can and should confront people.

In closing, discuss: **How can these insights from Jesus' example help you help your friends with drug and alcohol problems?**

Jesus and the Woman at the Well
John 4:4-36

◆ **BACKGROUND BYTES:** Most Jewish leaders regarded the Samaritans unclean and chose not to associate with them. The animosity was so intense that sometime around Jesus' birth, a group of Samaritans scattered bones in the Jewish temple during Passover.
• The woman at the well had another strike against her—she was a woman. In the culture of Jesus' day, women weren't respected. Jewish men like Jesus usually didn't speak to women alone in public.
• The woman went to the well in the heat of the day when no one else would be there, possibly because she had been scorned for her lifestyle in the past and wanted to avoid seeing anyone.

◆ **SCRIPTURE BYTES:** In the Old Testament, water is a familiar analogy for the law (see Proverbs 13:14, Jeremiah 17:13, Zechariah 14:8). The "gift" Jesus speaks of is certainly a relationship with God. • Not only is Jesus' message unique but His approach is equally significant. In the Old Testament, believers were often commanded to separate themselves from those who didn't believe what they believed. There are few examples of any Israelites reaching out with compassion to help those in need who were not associated with the faith (see 1 Kings 17:7-24 as one notable exception). It's important to note that Jesus didn't just offer the "living water" to the woman without also confronting her lifestyle.

◆ **BYTE-SIZE INSIGHTS:** Jesus didn't wait for us to reach out to Him, He came to where we were and offered the great gift of a relationship with God through the Jesus. The gift of "living water"—the "high" that never goes away—is available to all of us who trust in Jesus Christ.

CUSTOM CURRICULUM

STEP 4

What Not To Do

Below, students listen to roleplays on tape and evaluate the way the people on tape confronted their friends: 10-15 minutes.
Or, choose one of the option categories highlighted in the left sidebar and see pages 89-93 for more "Getting the Point" options.

OPTIONS

SMALL GROUP
LARGE GROUP
FELLOWSHIP & WORSHIP
MOSTLY GUYS
SHORT MEETING TIME

Supplies needed: cassette tape, tape player, copies of Resource 15, "To Do or Not to Do" (page 86), paper, pencils.
Set up: Ahead of time, recruit students to read the scenarios on Resource 15 onto cassette tape. (If you can't find a tape recorder, you can always just role play the scenarios "live.")

Tell students to pair off. Pass out paper and pencils. You might introduce this activity by saying something like: **You are going to hear three scenarios played on tape that reveal what not to do in terms of helping your friends who have drug and alcohol problems.** Play the scenarios from the tape. Have pairs respond to these two questions on their paper: **First, what did the confronter do wrong? Secondly, how would you do it differently to do it right?** Discuss students' answers to each situation one at a time.

SESSION FIVE

STEP 5

A Friend In Need . . .

Below, students pray for a friend struggling with drug or alcohol abuse and commit to pray for wisdom as they seek to confront him or her in love: 5-10 minutes.
Or, choose one of the option categories highlighted to the right (see pages 89-93 for more "Getting Personal" options).

OPTIONS
- EXTRA ACTION
- HEARD IT ALL BEFORE
- MOSTLY GIRLS
- MOSTLY GUYS
- EXTRA FUN
- JR. HIGH/HIGH SCHOOL COMBINED
- EXTRA CHALLENGE

Challenge each student to pray for one friend who's struggling with drug abuse. You might say something like: **Close your eyes and think of a friend you may have who is struggling with drug or alcohol abuse. I believe God will bring someone to your mind. Pray for your friend right now. Ask God to help them.** Leave about a minute of silence, but then take your challenge to students one step further. Challenge them to commit to God to put a confronting strategy into action. While students' heads are still bowed, you might say something like: **Are you willing to confront your friend? You may be God's best tool to help them. If you're willing to confront them, make a commitment that's just between you and God. Pray that God will give you wisdom and the right words to say. Pray that your friend will get some help.** Leave a few more minutes for silent prayer, then dismiss.

THE DRUG FREE CHALLENGE

Insight Cards

RESOURCE 14

When I read about how Jesus confronted someone in trouble, I think:	When I read about how Jesus confronted someone in trouble, I think:
When I read about how Jesus confronted someone in trouble, I think:	When I read about how Jesus confronted someone in trouble, I think:
When I read about how Jesus confronted someone in trouble, I think:	When I read about how Jesus confronted someone in trouble, I think:

THE DRUG FREE CHALLENGE
To Do Or Not To Do?

Scenario #1
Don't reject the person, reject the practice.

Friend: You know you have a pretty bad drug problem, Bill.

Bill: Yeah, I know, I know.

Friend: You're hanging around a bunch of losers lately.

Bill: Hey! Maybe they have problems you just don't understand.

Friend: All I understand is that you're going to be a loser too, Bill.

Bill: Who made you judge and jury of my life? I thought you were supposed to be my friend.

Friend: Not anymore, Bill. I am a Christian, and Christians don't hang around losers!

Scenario #2
Don't be afraid to confront directly and assertively; you might be saving a friend's life (or, "Don't beat around the bush").

Friend: Hey Steve, what are you going to do tonight?

Steve: Party and get drunk like I do every Saturday night. What else?

Friend: You don't want to do that!

Steve: Why not?

Friend: It's just not good for you, that's all.

Steve: Well neither are all those french fries you eat but I don't see you stopping that.

Friend: Oh, uhm, well, maybe next weekend you could come with me to a movie instead of a party.

Steve: Well maybe, but I think there's a party that might be funner.

Friend: Uh . . . I don't think "funner" is a word.

Steve: Hey why don't you come with me? It might loosen you up! You Christians are so uptight!

Friend: Well I don't think so. But try not to get drunk tonight, o.k.? Maybe next week we can do something together, okay?

Steve: Sure. Maybe.

Scenario #3
Have practical advice for your friends when you talk to them about their drug/alcohol problem.

Friend: Sue, I'm your friend and I'm really concerned about the drugs you've been doing. You've changed.

Sue: I know, you may be right, but I just can't seem to stop.

Friend: But you have to stop. Just don't do it anymore.

Sue: But you don't know how hard it is.

Friend: Maybe I don't, but you just have to!

Sue: How? I've tried. It never works.

Friend: I don't know . . . maybe you should talk to someone.

Sue: Like who?

Friend: How should I know? What about your parents?

Sue: Yeah, right!

Friend: Well, I don't know. There must be someone or something you can do to get help. Just pray to God.

Sue: I do pray, but it doesn't seem to help. I wish I knew what to do.

Friend: So do I.

THE DRUG FREE CHALLENGE
MIKE AND RYAN

optional RESOURCE 16

❶

Michael and Ryan had grown up together. Preschool, elementary school, Boy Scouts, youth group. They even went with each other on family vacations. And although their friendship had experienced ups and downs over the years, even as high school juniors they were still each other's best friends. Or, at least that's what they said.

But the truth was, ever since Michael made varsity football this year, he had begun to hang out more and more with the guys on the team. Michael was getting into a world that Ryan didn't want any part of: the party scene. It began with a party at the end of "hell week" last summer. Michael went and got drunk for the first time. Although he later repented at a youth group next weekend and decided to not do it again, little by little he was sucked back in. It began first with beer, then harder liquor, and then marijuana.

❷

For a long time, Ryan tried to talk to Michael about his partying. It was awkward for Ryan, especially because he was feeling abandoned by Michael and his new group of friends. But Ryan knew confronting his friend was the right thing to do.

"I know drinking isn't right," said Michael when Ryan first confronted him. But Michael continued to drink anyway. He justified his actions: "It's not like I'm an alcoholic," he said. "I've just always been such a straight kid. I'm just playing around a little. It's just for fun. Don't worry. I promise I'll stop as soon as football is over, OK?"

"Hey," Michael added as Ryan was walking out the door, "Thanks for checking up on me."

That last comment frustrated Ryan more than anything. He felt like Michael was patronizing him. What Ryan didn't realize was that Michael would remember Ryan's words. And just in time.

❸

Michael's team won the league championship that fall. Of course, the team held a huge party to celebrate. By 2 A.M., Michael was completely fried. He was wasted and half asleep. Michael's friend Brian offered to give Michael a ride home. "No, I'd better not go home like this," Michael said. Then he added, "See ya later."

But Michael never did see Brian later. Brian's car ran off the road. He was killed when his car hit the highway divider. He should have never been driving in his condition. Too much alcohol.

Michael was still hung over when he got the news that Brian was dead. Michael didn't even go home. He went straight to Ryan's. Ryan held his friend while Michael broke down and wept. He was broken thinking about Brian. He was broken thinking about his own life. How close he was to getting killed, also. How close he was to wasting his own life if he didn't do something about his problem. It was Ryan's words of confrontation that came back to him now. What he once patronized he now respected. Ryan had been the only one who cared enough to say something.

❹

Later that day, Ryan was right by Michael's side when he told his parents and their youth leader about his partying. He knew that Ryan didn't approve of his partying but he never doubted Ryan's commitment to him as a person. It was that support and accountability that gave Michael the strength to walk back to God.

OPTIONS

SESSION FIVE

EXTRA ACTION

STEP 2 - CONFRONT OR HIDE?
Toss a ball around a circle and discuss how to confront others in tough situations.

Stand in a circle. Start by naming a "sticky situation"—one that requires students to decide whether or not to confront someone Toss the ball to anyone in the circle. The student that catches the ball must share a response then toss the ball to a new person. Continue until every person gets an opportunity to answer. Examples of "sticky situations": your friend is struggling with drug abuse; your sister overslept her alarm and is about to be late; a senior at school is picking on a freshman. *(Needed: playground ball.)*

STEP 5 - COURAGE WAVE
Announce commitments and run through a "wave" of encouragement.

This activity will work any time you want to encourage your students. Use it here to encourage students in their commitments to confront and help peers struggling with drug or alcohol abuse. As directed in Step 5, have students choose a person to pray for and decide on a way they might confront that person. Divide your group into two groups and form straight lines with each group facing the other. Have students in the first group reach out and grab the hands of the students across from them in the second group. Give any student who wants the opportunity to stand in front of the two lines and, detail his or her confrontation strategy (for example, he or she might say something like, "I will confront John at school by. . . ."), and ask for accountability from the group. The student should then walk, jog, or run between the two lines. Students in the lines raise their arms just before the jogging student reaches them and lower their arms as soon as the jogging student has passed. Encourage all students to shout encouragement loudly as the student goes by.

SMALL GROUP

STEP 3 - WARM-UP QUESTIONS
Use this warm-up discussion to get students ready for the Bible study.

Discuss one or more of these warm-up questions that will help you build deeper community with your group and prepare them to hear the Bible Story: **Name a time when a friend confronted you. What happened? How did you respond? Then what? Name a time when you had to confront someone else. What happened? How did he or she respond? Then what? Name a time when you should have confronted a friend but didn't. What happened? Why do you wish you would have confronted your friend?** Use the Bible study and discussion questions as found in Step 3. Before moving on, return to the discussions you started at the beginning of this step and ask students: **How do you think Jesus would have responded to the situations we discussed earlier?** *(Needed: supplies listed in Step 3.)*

STEP 4 - ROLEPLAY w/ATTITUDE
Roleplay various styles of confrontation.

Set up a roleplay scenario where students will confront their best friend who is struggling with drug abuse. First, assign the role of the drug-abusing friend. Then give three students index cards on which you've written three different attitudes: "Angry and judgmental," "Overly understanding and sympathetic but not really confronting," and "Confronting with love but direct." Students who have the cards should take turns roleplaying a scene of confrontation while acting out the attitude their card describes. Keep this activity flowing rapidly but smoothly by stopping one roleplay before it gets old and starting a new one right after. Ask: **Which attitude of confrontation was most like Jesus' attitude when He confronted the woman at the well?** *(Needed: index cards, pens.)*

LARGE GROUP

STEP 3 - HELPING, JESUS' STYLE
Small groups study the Bible passage, then share with another small group.

For a more controlled and focused time of study, have students get in groups of three. If possible, match an upperclassman with two underclassmen. Give groups five to six minutes to list as many things as they can think of that Jesus did to help the Samaritan Woman, then give them another three to four minutes to share their answers with one other small group. If time allows, expand on the students' answers to emphasize the key points as directed in Step 3 in the main lesson. Then discuss: **How can these insights from Jesus' example help you confront your friends who struggle with drug and alcohol problems?** *(Needed: Bibles.)*

STEP 4 - WRITTEN RESPONSES
Write responses to the roleplays on index cards.

This variation will help you engage more students by giving them a writing activity to do while listening to the scenarios. Pass out index cards. When students listen to the taped scenarios from Resource 15 as directed in the main lesson, encourage them to write down a short note to the fictional character who was the confronter in the scenario. After each scenario, have students turn in the cards and read a handful of the responses. *(Needed: index cards, supplies listed in Step 4.)*

OPTIONS

SESSION FIVE

HEARD IT ALL BEFORE

STEP 3 - JESUS AT THE BAR
Write modern paraphrases of the story of Jesus and the woman at the well.

The lesson behind Jesus' encounter with the Samaritan woman is a universal one. It is as relevant today as it was in Bible times. Before you go into the discussion questions listed in Step 3, move your students into groups of two or three and have them rewrite the story in a modern setting. Encourage them to follow the story line from the Bible but to change details to place the encounter in your town or in a nearby city last week. Instruct each group to read its story to one other small group, then choose one or two to be read out loud to everyone. (Needed: supplies listed in Step 3.)

STEP 5 - ADOPT A FRIEND
Visit teens in a halfway house or other drug or alcohol program, then write encouraging letters.

Some church kids (especially those who are home schooled or attend a Christian school) may genuinely not have any friends or acquaintances with a drug or alcohol problem. If an organization in your community deals with families or individuals who struggle in this area, involve your students in a service project which will allow them to get to know some of the young people involved. Those kids can then become the focus of your students' prayers. If an off-site visit is impractical, ask the organization for names of adolescents that the kids in your group could write to and encourage. Coach your students not to be condescending or "preachy." If local agencies are hesitant to provide names, have your students write generic letters of encouragement and send them to a juvenile hall or prison to be posted for those who are struggling alone. (Needed: paper, pens.)

LITTLE BIBLE BACKGROUND

STEP 1 - JESUS AND THE SINNERS
Play "Would You Rather Hang with..." then discuss who Jesus "hung" with.

Instead of playing "Would You Rather," play "Who Would You Rather Hang With." Ask questions like: **Would you rather hang out with the President of the United States or Tom Cruise?** Students stand on the left wall to vote for the first choice and on the right wall to vote for the second. Continue the game comparing names of people your students are familiar with. Also compare homeless people with rich people, people of low repute with people of high repute, and so on. At the end of the game, switch gears and ask a true/false question: **Did Jesus hang out with people who drank too much?** The answer is almost certainly yes—Jesus hung out with prostitutes, the outcasts, and all sorts of people labeled "sinners" (for example, Matthew 9:10-13). Why? Because He loved them and He came to help them. Today Christians carry God's love to the lost. While it is in no way proper to join in the sins of sinners, it is also improper to hide the light of the Gospel from those who need it.

STEP 3 - STAGES OF DISCOVERY
Examine the process the woman at the well went through to understand Jesus.

Point out several steps the woman made in her understanding of who Jesus was. First, she recognized the He was a Jew (see John 4:9). This might be the same as a student's drug abusing friend saying, "You are a Christian." In verse 19, she came to see Jesus as a prophet. The student's friend might say, "You might be worth listening to." The woman eventually recognized Jesus as the Messiah (see verse 29). The student's friend might find the Savior just as the woman did. Encourage group members to see substance abuse as one indication that a person needs to be told about the love of God and the way to find peace in Jesus. (Needed: supplies listed in Step 3.)

FELLOWSHIP & WORSHIP

STEP 2 - WHO MADE YOU JUDGE?
Share experiences about judging and being judged.

Ask students to get into groups of three or four. Say: **Today we're going to talk about judging others. The person whose birthday is closest to today will go first. Share a time when you were judged or confronted (fairly or unfairly), or a time when you judged or confronted someone.** Tell students to relate their sharing to drugs and alcohol if possible. Encourage students to share as honestly. (Needed: bottles.)

STEP 4 - YOU'RE THERE!
Reflect, meditate, and imagine that you are in the Bible story.

Lead students in a guided meditation using John 21:15-17. Turn the lights down. Say: **Put yourself in the story. Imagine where Jesus and Peter are standing, what the scene looks like, smells like. How are Jesus and Peter feeling? Is anyone watching? What is the mood?** Read the story a second time and say: **Now pretend you are Peter in the story. How do you feel? Why are you responding the way you are?** Read the story a third time and say: **Now think about what it would be like to be Jesus. What kinds of things would be on your heart? What do you think of the way Jesus is expressing Himself?** When you've finished reading the passage through three times, challenge students to take a few minutes praying for a friend they feel they need to confront. Ask them to pray for opportunity, courage, and Christian love. (Needed: Bibles.)

OPTIONS

S E S S I O N   F I V E

STEP 1 - GATHER INFO
Network and gather resources from throughout your community.

It's important to get a list of local material/resources available to teenagers to deal with the topic of how best to say no to drugs and alcohol. Youth Service Bureaus and Community Service Agencies are great resources. This kind of information is particularly helpful when you discuss drugs and alcohol with girls because many girls struggle with self-esteem issues. Information you gather can help you teach your girls how to stand up for themselves.

STEP 5 - REMEMBER BEADS
Add beads to the PRAY bracelets that remind girls to pray for a friend.

If you made PRAY bracelets in Step 4 at the end of Session 2, you can close this series by giving girls two new beads to add to their bracelets. Bring in beads of many colors. Girls should pick one color bead to remind them of their own commitment to be drug free, then pick a second color to remind them to pray for any friends they know who struggle with drug or alcohol abuse. If you didn't make PRAY bracelets in Session 2, you can have girls make bracelets now having them string beads through thin pieces of leather. *(Needed: leather, beads.)*

STEP 4 - THE SILENT SYNDROME
Tape record, play, and discuss a fourth scenario that features a guy who is silent.

Because of the "coolness factor," many guys become silent about their friends' drinking or drug problems Add this scenario to those listed on Resource 15:

Kevin: Tonight's the night. My mom and dad are outta town. It's party time!
Rob: Oh . . . What are you going to do?
Kevin: We got a couple of college guys to buy a keg for us. We're going to get trashed.
Rob: Yeah . . . I guess I'm just going to go over to Jen's house and watch a movie.
Kevin: Hey dude . . . Why don't you come over? It'll be totally cool. You never know, you may even get a buzz!
Rob: No, we're supposed to watch some movie. You know, crying, love, sensitivity, and all that.
Kevin: Whatever. All I know is I'm going to party tonight!
Rob: Yeah. OK. See ya Monday.

(Needed: supplies listed in Step 4.)

STEP 5 - PRAYER AND ACTION
Challenge pairs of guys not just to pray for but to reach out to friends in need.

Have students get with one or two other guys they know pretty well. Have the teams huddle together and think of two guys who struggle with drugs and alcohol. If possible, teams should try to think of guys whom all team members know. Challenge teams to come up with a strategy to confront in love the two guys they prayed for. Help teams set specific, measurable goals; for example: Two weeks from now I will have let Mark know that I care about him and I don't want to see him destroy his life on drugs. Finally, have the teams commit to praying for their guys once every day alone and once every other day (on the phone if they have to) as a team.

STEP 2 - PASS THE ROLE
This twist on roleplaying gets all—or almost all—students involved.

Start a roleplay by assigning one student to play the role of Teen 1: he is struggling with the fact that he likes the buzz he gets from alcohol; he is wondering if he wouldn't get a better buzz from trying a harder drug. Next assign the role of Teen 2, a long-time friend of Teen 1. Teen 2 is active in her youth ministry, committed to God, and sometimes labeled a "goodie-goodie." Give the first pair a few minutes to get the discussion going, then assign Teen 1 to a new student—instead of starting the roleplay over, have him jump right in and take over. Encourage the new student to take the conversation in a slightly new direction as he deems appropriate. After a few more minutes, replace Teen 2 as well. Continue to substitute like this as time permits. What you end up with is a roleplay that allows almost all the teens to participate and voice what they would do in a particular situation. Discuss: **What do you wish had been said but wasn't? What would you say differently next time? How hard is it to talk about God and His role in a struggle with drugs and alcohol? As "Teen 2" was it hard not to be "preachy"? What did you learn about how to (and how not to) talk to friends about drugs and alcohol?**

STEP 5 - FOLLOW-UP FUN NIGHT
Plan a fun time when students can get together and celebrate their commitments.

Close your series on drugs and alcohol by taking a few minutes to plan a special night of fun when you can honor and celebrate students' "drug free" commitments. You might throw a party or take your students to a special dinner at the end of the school year. Students will be motivated by having something fun to which they can look forward.

OPTIONS

SESSION FIVE

STEP 2 - STORY ON TAPE
Videotape the "Mike and Ryan" story.

The optional Resource 16, "Mike and Ryan" (page 87), is a story that can be read in four parts. You can break after each part to discuss what the characters should do next and what the difference is between confronting in love and confronting with judging. Add a visual component to this story by getting two talented actors to act it out on video for you ahead of time. Pause the video after each section of the story and discuss: **Should Ryan confront Michael? Why or why not? How should he confront Michael? Is Ryan judging Michael if he confronts him? Why or why not? How can Ryan confront Michael without judging him?** *(Needed: TV, VCR, video camera, blank tape, copies of Resource 16).*

STEP 3 - SILENT MOVIES
Small groups make silent movies of the story of Jesus and the woman at the well.

To engage teens in the Bible study, have groups of four to six students read and act out John 4:1-26 without using words. Actors will have to think of creative hand signs and other ways to communicate the events of the story. Film these "silent movies." When you play them back, ask students to fill out the "Insight Cards" as directed in Step 3. Continue with the discussion as directed in the main lesson. *(Needed: TV, VCR, video camera, blank tape.)*

STEP 2 - MIKE AND RYAN
Read optional Resource 16.

The optional Resource 16, "Mike and Ryan" (page 87) is a story that can be read in four parts. You can break after each part to discuss what the characters should do next and what the difference is between confronting in love and confronting with judging. Pause the reading of the story after each section and discuss: **Should Ryan confront Michael? Why or why not? How should he confront Michael? Is Ryan judging Michael if he confronts him? Why or why not? How can Ryan confront Michael without judging him?** *(Needed: copies of Resource 16).*

STEP 3 - CUT TO THE CHASE
Skip some discussion of students' insights.

If you don't have time to discuss what students wrote on their "Insight Cards" in depth, have students to turn to one or two other people next to them and share their insights. But be sure to review for the students the specific insights outlined in the main text. *(Needed: supplies listed in Step 3.)*

STEP 4 - IT ONLY TAKES ONE
Discuss just one taped scenario from Resource 15.

If you don't have time to discuss all the roleplay situations listed on Resource 15, tape and discuss only the first scenario. Follow the rest of the directions in Step 4, but add this question: **What are some other examples of things you should *not* do when you confront others?** *(Needed: supplies listed in Step 4.)*

STEP 2 - SPIRIT E-MAIL
Use an "electronic" analogy to discuss how God speaks to teens.

Many city teens often feel like God overlooks their problems. They feel hopeless. To help teens see God hasn't given up on them, be as practical as you can about how God communicates to Christians. If your students will relate to the analogy, explain that making Jesus Lord is like owning a top-rated computer with the fastest baud speed—God is always sending us "e-mail" from His Spirit to us. The Spirit e-mail we get is usually in one of these "E" categories:
1) Endorsing Spirit E-mail —Asks the believer to do something; called a prompting.
2) Encouraging Spirit E-mail —Empowers the believer to continue growing in an area desired.
3) Enforcing Spirit E-mail—Convicts the believer he or she should *not* do something.
4) Encrypted Spirit E-mail—A private message concerning God's will and plan for the believer's life.
5) Emergency Spirit-E-mail —Asks for the believer's practical and immediate action or reaction to a situation at hand.
Discuss: **Do you know any friends with a drug or alcohol problem? Is God sending you any "e-mails" about that? What is He saying?**

STEP 3 - TODAY'S LEPERS
Study how Jesus treated lepers.

In addition to or instead of reading the story of the woman at the well, study the story of the ten lepers (Luke 17:12-21). Analyze the passage with the same questions given in the main lesson concerning how Jesus treated the woman at the well. City teens can relate to the rejection associated with leprosy. They will learn that even though they are sometimes treated like "lepers" by society, Jesus doesn't look down on them. *(Needed: Bibles.)*

OPTIONS

SESSION FIVE

STEP 3 - PAUSE BUTTON
Pause during the Bible story and discuss how Jesus might confront the woman.

This idea is a little more active and will help engage students in the Bible study. Ask for three volunteers to read John 4:1-26—one student should read the part of the narrator, another all the lines Jesus has to say, and a third all the woman's lines. After reading up to verse 15, "press the pause button." Discuss: **We'll soon find out the woman had some "secret sins." What would Jesus say to the woman if He wanted to both judge her and confront her? What would Jesus say to the woman if He wanted to confront her with love and not judgement?** Have the three volunteers continue reading John 4:16-26 according to their parts. You can then either complete Resource 14 in small groups or prepare two students to give two-minute summaries of their "insights"—but have them present the information in a casual and conversational manner. *(Needed: supplies listed in Step 3.)*

STEP 5 - OFFER IT UP
"Offer" students who struggle with drugs and alcohol to God.

To make the concluding step more concrete, ask students to tangibly offer a friend to God. After students pray for their friends as directed in the main lesson, ask them to write their friend's first initial on an index card. Have them fold the index card in half so that no one else can see the letter that they have written. Pass around offering baskets and ask students to place their index cards in the baskets as an offering to God and a symbol of their commitment to pray, confront, and love the person represented by the index card. Make it clear that no one will ever see the index cards, and that you personally will throw them in the trash after the session ends. *(Needed: index cards, supplies listed in Step 3.)*

STEP 3 - GODLY CONFRONTATION
Study Philippians 2:1-11 as a confrontation guide.

In addition to or instead of the Bible study in Step 3 in the main lesson, read Philippians 2:1-11. Based on these verses make a "To Do" list and a "To Don't" list that can work as guidelines for godly confrontation. For example, list "Have a servant's heart" on the "do" side and "Be condescending" on the "don't" side. "Tell students to bow their heads and reflect on the following questions as you read them slowly: *(Needed: Bibles.)*

STEP 5 - DECISION JOURNAL
Challenge students to keep a Journal to track their "inward decisions."

Make "Inward Decision Journals" by folding card stock paper in half down the middle. On top of the left-hand side write "Other" and on top of the right-hand side write "Self." Challenge students to record times they remember to make others-centered decisions in the coming week and write a brief description down in the appropriate column. Most will discover that when they think about being others-centered they tend to put it into practice more as well. *(Needed: card stock paper, pens.)*

STEP 1 (5-10 MIN. UNLESS NOTED)
- ❏ **Little Bible:** Jesus and the Sinners
- ❏ **Mostly Girls:** Gather Info

STEP 2 (10-15 MIN. UNLESS NOTED)
- ❏ **Extra Action:** Confront or Hide?
- ❏ **Fellowship & Worship:** Who Made You Judge?
- ❏ **Extra Fun:** Pass the Role
- ❏ **Media:** Story on Tape
- ❏ **Short Time:** Mike and Ryan (5-10 min.)
- ❏ **Urban:** Spirit E-Mail

STEP 3 (15-20 MIN. UNLESS NOTED)
- ❏ **Small Group:** Warm-up Questions
- ❏ **Large Group:** Helping, Jesus' Style
- ❏ **Heard It All:** Jesus at the Bar
- ❏ **Little Bible:** Stages of Discovery
- ❏ **Media:** Silent Movies
- ❏ **Short Time:** Cut to the Chase (10-15 min.)
- ❏ **Urban:** Today's Lepers
- ❏ **Combined:** Pause Button
- ❏ **Extra Challenge:** Godly Confrontation

STEP 4 (10-15 MIN. UNLESS NOTED)
- ❏ **Small Group:** Roleplay w/Attitude
- ❏ **Large Group:** Written Responses
- ❏ **Fellowship & Worship:** You're There!
- ❏ **Mostly Guys:** The Silent Syndrome
- ❏ **Short Time:** It Only Takes One (5-10 min.)

STEP 5 (5-10 MIN. UNLESS NOTED)
- ❏ **Extra Action:** Courage Wave
- ❏ **Heard It All:** Adopt a Friend
- ❏ **Mostly Girls:** Remember Beads
- ❏ **Mostly Guys:** Prayer and Action
- ❏ **Extra Fun:** Follow-up Fun Night
- ❏ **Combined:** Offer It Up
- ❏ **Extra Challenge:** Decision Journal

Other Custom Curriculum Titles

High School

Beliefs to Beware of — Straight Answers about Cults

Can't Help It? — How to Quit Bad Habits and Start Good Ones

Free Gifts for Everybody! — Discovering Your Spiritual Gifts

Going Against the Flow — When Being a Christian Feels Weird

Hormone Helper — Getting Along as a Guy or Girl

Is Anybody There? — Reaching for a Real Relationship with God

Streetwise — Great Advice from Proverbs and Ecclesiastes

The Whole Story — Things They Don't Tell You in School about Sex, and More!

They're Not Like Us! — What Different Churches Believe

Too Tough? — The Hardest Teachings of Jesus

Unseen Mysteries — A Behind-the-Scenes Look at Angels, Demons, and More

What Do You Think? — Measuring Your Opinions against the Bible

What, Me Holy? — Staying Clean in a Grungy World

Your Bible's Alive — How to Get Friendly with God's Book

You've Got Style — Choosing Your Music, Clothes, and Attitude

Junior High/Middle School

Basic Training — Things Every Christian Kid Should Know

Bouncing Back — What to Do after Mistakes, Embarrassment, and Other Daily Disasters

Extreme Closeup — How You and God Can Stay Connected

Extreme Friendship — Mind-Blowing Ideas about Friendship from Jesus' Own Life

Face to Face with Jesus — What He's Really Like

Gotta Have It? — How to Get What You Need and Forget What You Don't

In the Beginning ... What? — The Bible Talks about Creation

Just Look at You — Feeling Good about the Way You're Made

New Testament Speedway — A Zip through the New Testament

Old Testament Speedway — A Zip through the Old Testament

Parent Pains — Bringing Some Peace to Your Place

Riding Those Mood Swings — What to Do with Up-and-Down Feelings

Tongue Untwisters — Keeping Your Mouth from Getting You in Trouble

What Would Jesus Do? — Making the Best Choices

Which Way to God? — What Other Religions Believe

Why Be a Christian? — Deciding Whether It's Worth Following Jesus

To order, call David C. Cook Ministry Resources at 1-800-323-7543 (U.S.)
In Canada call 1-800-263-2664

Custom Curriculum Critique

Please take a moment to fill out this evaluation form, rip it out, fold it, tape it, and send it back to us. This will help us continue to customize products for you. Thanks!

1. Overall, please give this *Custom Curriculum* course (*Extreme Friendship*) a grade in terms of how well it worked for you. (A=excellent; B=above average; C=average; D=below average; F=failure) Circle one.

    A   B   C   D   F

2. Now assign a grade to each part of this curriculum that you used.

a.	Upfront article	A	B	C	D	F	Didn't use
b.	Publicity Clip art	A	B	C	D	F	Didn't use
c.	Resource Sheets	A	B	C	D	F	Didn't use
d.	Session 1	A	B	C	D	F	Didn't use
e.	Session 2	A	B	C	D	F	Didn't use
f.	Session 3	A	B	C	D	F	Didn't use
g.	Session 4	A	B	C	D	F	Didn't use
h.	Session 5	A	B	C	D	F	Didn't use

3. How helpful were the options?
    - ❏ Very helpful
    - ❏ Somewhat helpful
    - ❏ Not too helpful
    - ❏ Not at all helpful

4. Rate the amount of options:
    - ❏ Too many
    - ❏ About the right amount
    - ❏ Too few

5. Tell us how often you used each type of option (4=Always; 3=Sometimes; 2=Seldom; 1=Never)

	4	3	2	1
Extra Action	❏	❏	❏	❏
Combined Jr. High/High School	❏	❏	❏	❏
Urban	❏	❏	❏	❏
Small Group	❏	❏	❏	❏
Large Group	❏	❏	❏	❏
Extra Fun	❏	❏	❏	❏
Heard It All Before	❏	❏	❏	❏
Little Bible Background	❏	❏	❏	❏
Short Meeting Time	❏	❏	❏	❏
Fellowship and Worship	❏	❏	❏	❏
Mostly Guys	❏	❏	❏	❏
Mostly Girls	❏	❏	❏	❏
Media	❏	❏	❏	❏
Extra Challenge (High School only)	❏	❏	❏	❏
Sixth Grade (Jr. High/M.S. only)	❏	❏	❏	❏

NAME_____
STREET_____
CITY_____
STATE_____ ZIP _____

|||||

```
NO POSTAGE
NECESSARY
IF MAILED
IN THE
UNITED STATES
```

BUSINESS REPLY MAIL
FIRST CLASS MAIL PERMIT NO.720 COLORADO SPRINGS, CO

POSTAGE WILL BE PAID BY ADDRESSEE

David C. Cook Church Ministries
ATTN: YOUTH DEPT.
4050 LEE VANCE VIEW
COLORADO SPRINGS, CO   80918-9951

(tape here)

---

6. What did you like best about this course?

7. What suggestions do you have for improving Custom Curriculum?

8. Other topics you'd like to see covered in this series:

9. Are you?
    - ❏ Full-time, paid youthworker
    - ❏ Part-time, paid youthworker
    - ❏ Volunteer youthworker

10. When did you use Custom Curriculum?
    - ❏ Sunday School   ❏ Small Group
    - ❏ Youth Group   ❏ Retreat
    - ❏ Other

---

11. What grades did you use it with? _____
12. How many kids used the curriculum in an average week? _____
13. What's the approximate attendance of your entire Sunday school program (Nursery through Adult)? _____
14. If you would like information on other Custom Curriculum courses, or other youth products from Cook Ministry Resources, please fill out the following:

    Name: _____
    Church Name: _____
    Address: _____
    _____
    Phone: (____) _____

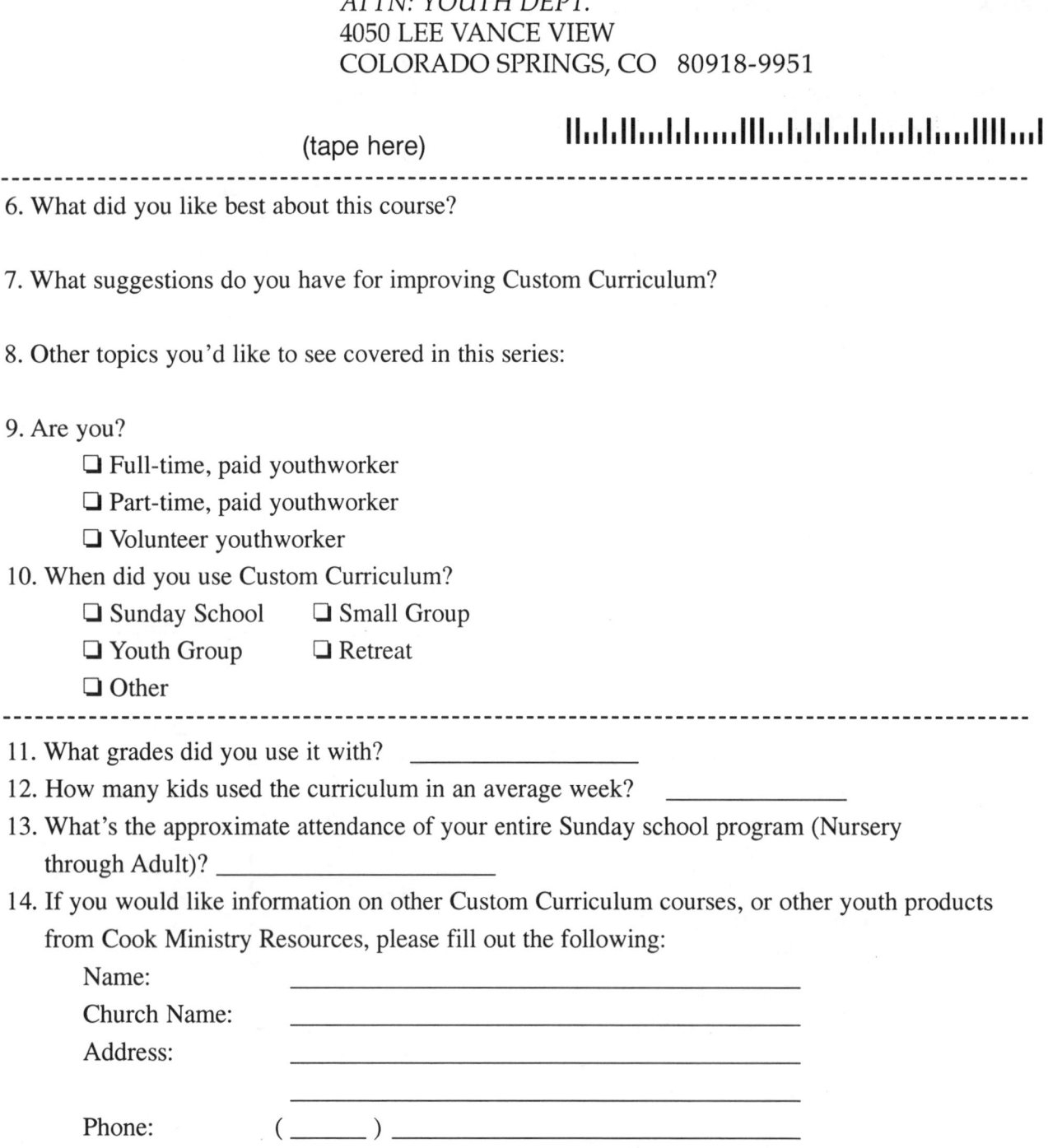

Thank you!